MILTON STUDIES INDEX
I–XII

MILTON STUDIES
James D. Simmonds, Editor

MILTON STUDIES. INDEX ❧

Volumes I-XII

Beth E. Luey

UNIVERSITY OF PITTSBURGH PRESS

Library of Congress Catalog Card Number 69-12335
ISBN 0-8229-3174-5 (Volume I) (out of print)
ISBN 0-8229-3194-x (Volume II)
ISBN 0-8229-3218-0 (Volume III)
ISBN 0-8229-3244-x (Volume IV)
ISBN 0-8229-3272-5 (Volume V)
ISBN 0-8229-3288-1 (Volume VI)
ISBN 0-8229-3305-5 (Volume VII)
ISBN 0-8229-3310-1 (Volume VIII)
ISBN 0-8229-3329-2 (Volume IX)
ISBN 0-8229-3356-x (Volume X)
ISBN 0-8229-3373-x (Volume XI)
ISBN 0-8229-3376-4 (Volume XII)
ISBN 0-8229-3389-6 (Index, I–XII)
US ISSN 0076-8820
Published by the University of Pittsburgh Press, Pittsburgh, Pa. 15260
Copyright © 1980, University of Pittsburgh Press
Feffer & Simons, Inc., London
Manufactured in the United States of America

The compiler is grateful to James D. Simmonds, Editor of *Milton Studies*,
for his advice and assistance in preparing this index.

CONTENTS

c·l

EXPLANATORY NOTES

THIS INDEX is divided into two sections. The first is a subject listing of articles in the first twelve volumes of *Milton Studies*. A reader who wants to know which articles discuss *Animadversions,* for example, or landscape, may simply look under those headings for a chronological list of essays that treat those subjects in some detail. The headings are in alphabetical order. Readers who have a more specific subject in mind, or who want a more detailed breakdown of a topic, should consult the index itself. If, for example, you want references to heroism in *Animadversions,* landscape in *Lycidas,* or trees, you will find these in the index. In both sections, roman numerals indicate the volume; arabic numbers, the pages.

Only three abbreviations are used: *PL* for *Paradise Lost, PR* for *Paradise Regained,* and *SA* for *Samson Agonistes.* Some other titles have been shortened. When alternative titles exist, cross-references are provided; if the list is brief, it is simply repeated.

Titles of works are indexed by their authors—*Faerie Queene* under "Spenser, Edmund," *Poetics* under "Aristotle," Corinthians under "Paul, St.," and so forth. The exceptions are works whose authors are not known and works by John Milton. These are indexed by title. Works by Milton with foreign titles are alphabetized under the first main word of the foreign title; cross-references are given for English titles if commonly used. For example, *De Doctrina Christiana* is alphabetized under *Doctrina;* the reader who looks under *Christian Doctrine* or *Of Christian Doctrine* will find a cross-reference. English titles are also alphabetized by the first main word: *On the Death of a Fair Infant* is in the Ds. The sonnets are numbered according to the listing in *John Milton, Complete Poems and Major Prose,* ed. Merritt Y. Hughes (New York, 1957) and are indexed as *Sonnet 1* and so on.

The entry for Milton is limited for the most part to biographical topics. His works, again, are listed by title, and his thoughts on various subjects are listed under those subjects (for example, "rhetoric" and "eternal torment"). Milton's critics and commentators are listed under

their names only, so that a reader interested in Barbara Lewalski's comments on *Paradise Regained* must look under "Lewalski, Barbara K.," not *"Paradise Regained."* If an author has had an article published in *Milton Studies,* its location is the first entry after his or her name and is italicized.

The articles in *Milton Studies* vary greatly in their specificity. Some cover the theory of literary criticism in ten pages, whereas others spend thirty pages on part of a sonnet. Thus, the index also varies greatly in level of specificity. There are entries for single words ("fondly," "stand"), for objects ("two-handed engine"), and for events ("Puritan revolution," "War in Heaven")—along with names, works by Milton and others, characters, and subjects ranging from insects to truth. If you are interested in a single word or concept, look for it first. If it is not there, move up the scale of generality. "Chrysanthemum" is not listed, but "flowers" is, complete with references to other entries which in turn lead further.

There is more repetition in this index than in most, but this seemed preferable to making it difficult or impossible to find a topic that could be indexed in several different ways. Thus, the reader seeking references to the biblical sources of *Paradise Lost* will find either a listing or a cross-reference under *"Paradise Lost:* biblical sources of" and "Genesis, Book of: as source for *PL*" (as well as other relevant portions of the Bible).

The purpose of this index, like any other, is to make it easier for readers to find what they are looking for, and I certainly hope it will do that. I also hope that it will lead readers to things they were *not* looking for—links they hadn't noticed, or passages they hadn't thought of before in quite the same connection.

MILTON STUDIES INDEX
I–XII

ARTICLES BY SUBJECT

L'Allegro and Il Penseroso

Leonora Leet Brodwin, "Milton and the Renaissance Circe," VI, 21–83.
Stanley E. Fish, "What It's Like to Read *L'Allegro* and *Il Penseroso*," VII, 77–99.
Stephen C. Behrendt, "Bright Pilgrimage: William Blake's Designs for *L'Allegro* and *Il Penseroso*," VIII, 123–47.
Norman B. Council, "*L'Allegro, Il Penseroso,* and 'The Cycle of Universal Knowledge,'" IX, 203–19.

Animadversions

D. M. Rosenberg, "Parody of Style in Milton's Polemics," II, 113–18.
John A. Via, "Milton's Antiprelatical Tracts: The Poet Speaks in Prose," V, 87–127.
Annabel Patterson, "The Civic Hero in Milton's Prose," VIII, 71–101.
James Egan, "Milton and the Marprelate Tradition," VIII, 103–21.

An Apology for Smectymnuus

D. M. Rosenberg, "Parody of Style in Milton's Polemics," II, 113–18.
John A. Via, "Milton's Antiprelatical Tracts: The Poet Speaks in Prose," V, 87–127.
Leonora Leet Brodwin, "Milton and the Renaissance Circe," VI, 21–83.
Annabel Patterson, "The Civic Hero in Milton's Prose," VIII, 71–101.

Areopagitica

Joseph Anthony Wittreich, Jr., "Milton's *Areopagitica:* Its Isocratic and Ironic Contexts," IV, 101–15.
Anne B. Long, "'She May Have More Shapes than One': Milton and the Modern Idea That Truth Changes," VI, 85–99.
B. Rajan, "The Cunning Resemblance," VII, 29–48.
Annabel Patterson, "The Civic Hero in Milton's Prose," VIII, 71–101.

3

Harry R. Smallenburg, "Contiguities and Moving Limbs: Style as Argument in *Areopagitica*," IX, 169–84.

Juanita Whitaker, " 'The Wars of Truth': Wisdom and Strength in *Areopagitica*," IX, 185–201.

The Art of Logic

Gordon Campbell, "*De Doctrina Christiana:* Its Structural Principles and Its Unfinished State," IX, 243–60.

Biblical and Rabbinical Sources

John T. Shawcross, "*Paradise Lost* and the Theme of Exodus," II, 3–26.

Kitty Cohen, "Milton's God in Council and War," III, 159–84.

Samuel S. Stollman, "Milton's Samson and the Jewish Tradition," III, 185–200.

Samuel S. Stollman, "Milton's Rabbinical Readings and Fletcher," IV, 195–215.

Emory Elliott, "Milton's Biblical Style in *Paradise Regained*," VI, 227–41.

Ernst Häublein, "Milton's Paraphrase of Genesis: A Stylistic Reading of *Paradise Lost*, Book VII," VII, 101–25.

Michael Lieb, "*Paradise Lost* and the Myth of Prohibition," VII, 233–65.

Mother M. Christopher Pecheux, "The Dread Voice in *Lycidas*," IX, 221–41.

John N. Wall, Jr., "The Contrarious Hand of God: *Samson Agonistes* and the Biblical Lament," XII, 117–39.

Biography

John T. Shawcross, "Milton and Diodati: An Essay in Psychodynamic Meaning," VII, 127–63.

John Spencer Hill, "Poet-Priest: Vocational Tension in Milton's Early Development," VIII, 41–69.

Earl Miner, "Dryden's Admired Acquaintance, Mr. Milton," XI, 3–27.

Robert Thomas Fallon, "Filling the Gaps: New Perspectives on Mr. Secretary Milton," XII, 165–95.

Mother M. Christopher Pecheux, "Milton and *Kairos*," XII, 197–211.

Classical and Mythological Sources

Mario A. Di Cesare, "*Paradise Lost* and Epic Tradition," I, 31–50.

Irene Samuel, "Milton and the Ancients on the Writing of History," II, 131–48.

Edwin B. Benjamin, "Milton and Tacitus," IV, 117–40.

Leonora Leet Brodwin, "Milton and the Renaissance Circe," VI, 21–83.

Carole S. Kessner, "Milton's Hebraic Herculean Hero," VI, 243–58.

Michael Lieb, "*Paradise Lost* and the Myth of Prohibition," VII, 233–65.

Don Parry Norford, "The Sacred Head: Milton's Solar Mysticism," IX, 37–75.

C. A. Patrides, "The Comic Dimension in Greek Tragedy and *Samson Agonistes*," X, 3–21.

E. R. Gregory, "Three Muses and a Poet: A Perspective on Milton's Epic Thought," X, 35–64.

Kurt Heinzelman, " 'Cold Consolation': The Art of Milton's Last Sonnet," X, 111–25.

John Spencer Hill, " 'Alcestis from the Grave': Image and Structure in *Sonnet XXIII*," X, 127–39.

Don Parry Norford, "The Separation of the World Parents in *Paradise Lost*," XII, 3–24.

Comus

Barbara Breasted, "*Comus* and the Castlehaven Scandal," III, 201–24.

Franklin R. Baruch, "Milton's *Comus*: Skill, Virtue, and Henry Lawes," V, 289–308.

Leonora Leet Brodwin, "Milton and the Renaissance Circe," VI, 21–83.

Alice-Lyle Scoufos, "The Mysteries in Milton's *Masque*," VI, 113–42.

Terry Kidner Kohn, "Landscape in the Transcendent Masque," VI, 143–64.

Thomas O. Calhoun, "On John Milton's *A Mask at Ludlow*," VI, 165–79.

B. Rajan, "The Cunning Resemblance," VII, 29–48.

John T. Shawcross, "'Milton and Diodati: An Essay in Psychodynamic Meaning," VII, 127–63.

John Spencer Hill, "Poet-Priest: Vocational Tension in Milton's Early Development," VIII, 41–69.

Don Parry Norford, "The Sacred Head: Milton's Solar Mysticism," IX, 37–75.

The Defences

Edwin B. Benjamin, "Milton and Tacitus," IV, 117–40.

Annabel Patterson, "The Civic Hero in Milton's Prose," VIII, 71–101.

The Divorce Tracts

Samuel S. Stollman, "Milton's Rabbinical Readings and Fletcher," IV, 195–215.

Theodore L. Huguelet, "The Rule of Charity in Milton's Divorce Tracts," VI, 199–214.

James Egan, "Milton and the Marprelate Tradition," VIII, 103–21.

John M. Perlette, "Milton, Ascham, and the Rhetoric of the Divorce Controversy," X, 195–215.

De Doctrina Christiana

O. B. Hardison, Jr., "Written Records and Truths of Spirit in *Paradise Lost*," I, 147–65.

Michael Lieb, "Milton and the Organicist Polemic," IV, 79–99.

Anne B. Long, " 'She May Have More Shapes than One': Milton and the Modern Idea That Truth Changes," VI, 85–99.

Leonora Leet Brodwin, "The Dissolution of Satan in *Paradise Lost*: A Study of Milton's Heretical Eschatology," VIII, 165–207.

Gordon Campbell, "*De Doctrina Christiana*: Its Structural Principles and Its Unfinished State," IX, 243–60.

Eikonoklastes

Annabel Patterson, "The Civic Hero in Milton's Prose," VIII, 71–101.

Elegies 1 and 6

Leonora Leet Brodwin, "Milton and the Renaissance Circe," VI, 21–83.

Epitaphium Damonis

John A. Via, "Milton's Antiprelatical Tracts: The Poet Speaks in Prose," V, 87–127.

John T. Shawcross, "Milton and Diodati: An Essay in Psychodynamic Meaning," VII, 127–63.

Historical Influences

Barbara Breasted, "*Comus* and the Castlehaven Scandal," III, 201–24.

Jackie Di Salvo, " 'The Lord's Battells': *Samson Agonistes* and the Puritan Revolution," IV, 39–62.

Stella P. Revard, "Milton's Gunpowder Poems and Satan's Conspiracy," IV, 63–77.

Keith W. Stavely, "The Style and Structure of Milton's *Readie and Easie Way*," V, 269–87.

Malcolm Kelsall, "The Historicity of *Paradise Regained*," XII, 35–51.

History

Irene Samuel, "Milton and the Ancients on the Writing of History," II, 131–48.

Edwin B. Benjamin, "Milton and Tacitus," IV, 117–40.

History of Britain

Edwin B. Benjamin, "Milton and Tacitus," IV, 117–40.

Landscape

John R. Knott, Jr., "Symbolic Landscape in *Paradise Lost*," II, 37–58.
Charlotte F. Otten, " 'My Native Element': Milton's Paradise and English Gardens," V, 249–67.
Terry Kidner Kohn, "Landscape in the Transcendent Masque," VI, 143–64.
G. Stanley Koehler, "Milton and the Art of Landscape," VIII, 3–40.

Lycidas

Kathleen M. Swaim, "Retributive Justice in *Lycidas:* The Two-Handed Engine," II, 119–29.
Donald M. Friedman, "*Lycidas:* The Swain's Paideia," III, 3–34.
Stewart A. Baker, "Milton's Uncouth Swain," III, 35–53.
William G. Riggs, "The Plant of Fame in *Lycidas*," IV, 151–61.
John A. Via, "Milton's Antiprelatical Tracts: The Poet Speaks in Prose," V, 87–127.
John Spencer Hill, "Poet-Priest: Vocational Tension in Milton's Early Development," VIII, 41–69.
Mother M. Christopher Pecheux, "The Dread Voice in *Lycidas*," IX, 221–41.

Methodology

Albert C. Labriola and Michael Lieb, "Preface," VII, vii–xii.
John M. Steadman, "The Epic as Pseudomorph: Methodology in Milton Studies," VII, 3–27.
Stanley E. Fish, "What It's Like to Read *L'Allegro* and *Il Penseroso*," VII, 77–99.
Burton J. Weber, "The Non-Narrative Approaches to *Paradise Lost:* A Gentle Remonstrance," IX, 77–103.

Milton's Influence

B. Rajan, "Introduction: The Varieties of Presence," XI, vii–xiv.
Earl Miner, "Dryden's Admired Acquaintance, Mr. Milton," XI, 3–27.
Barbara K. Lewalski, "On Looking Into Pope's Milton," XI, 29–50.
Joseph Anthony Wittreich, Jr., "Blake's Milton: 'To Immortals, . . . a Mighty Angel,' " XI, 51–82.

Edna Newmeyer, "Wordsworth on Milton and the Devil's Party," XI, 83–98.

Douglas Bush, "The Milton of Keats and Arnold," XI, 99–114.

B. Rajan, "Milton and Eliot: A Twentieth-Century Acknowledgment," XI, 115–29.

Nativity Ode

Lawrence W. Hyman, "Christ's Nativity and the Pagan Deities," II, 103–12.

Lawrence W. Kingsley, "Mythic Dialectic in the Nativity Ode," IV, 163–76.

Philip Rollinson, "Milton's Nativity Poem and the Decorum of Genre," VII, 165–88.

Paradise Lost

B. Rajan, "*Paradise Lost:* The Providence of Style," I, 1–14.

Thomas Kranidas, "A View of Milton and the Traditional," I, 15–29.

Mario A. Di Cesare, "*Paradise Lost* and Epic Tradition," I, 31–50.

John M. Steadman, "Milton's Rhetoric: Satan and the 'Unjust Discourse,' " I, 67–92.

Arnold Stein, "Satan's Metamorphoses: The Internal Speech," I, 93–113.

Anthony Low, "Angels and Food in *Paradise Lost*," I, 135–45.

O. B. Hardison, Jr., "Written Records and Truths of Spirit in *Paradise Lost*," I, 147–65.

Michael Fixler, "Milton's Passionate Epic," I, 167–92.

John T. Shawcross, "*Paradise Lost* and the Theme of Exodus," II, 3–26.

Leslie Brisman, "Serpent Error: *Paradise Lost* X, 216–18," II, 27–35.

John R. Knott, Jr., "Symbolic Landscape in *Paradise Lost*," II, 37–58.

William G. Riggs, "The Poet and Satan in *Paradise Lost*," II, 59–82.

Sherman H. Hawkins, "Samson's Catharsis," II, 211–30.

Albert R. Cirillo, "Tasso's *Il Mondo Creato:* Providence and the Created Universe," III, 83–102.

Lee A. Jacobus, "Self-Knowledge in *Paradise Lost:* Conscience and Contemplation," III, 103–18.

Thomas H. Blackburn, " 'Uncloister'd Virtue': Adam and Eve in Milton's Paradise," III, 119–37.

Sister Mary Brian Durkin, "Iterative Figures and Images in *Paradise Lost,* XI–XII," III, 139–58.

Kitty Cohen, "Milton's God in Council and War," III, 159–84.

Marcia Landy, "Kinship and the Role of Women in *Paradise Lost*," IV, 3–18.

Anthony Low, "Milton's God: Authority in *Paradise Lost*," IV, 19–38.

Stella P. Revard, "Milton's Gunpowder Poems and Satan's Conspiracy," IV, 63–77.

Roger B. Rollin, "*Paradise Lost:* 'Tragical—Comical—Historical—Pastoral,' " V, 3–37.

Gary M. McCown, "Milton and the Epic Epithalamium," V, 39–66.

Lee M. Johnson, "Milton's Blank Verse Sonnets," V, 129–53.

Kathleen M. Swaim, "Flower, Fruit, and Seed: A Reading of *Paradise Lost*," V, 155–76.

Jonathan Goldberg, "*Virga Iesse:* Analogy, Typology, and Anagogy in a Miltonic Simile," V, 177–90.

Thomas H. Blackburn, "Paradises Lost and Found: The Meaning and Function of the 'Paradise Within' in *Paradise Lost*," V, 191–211.

Jun Harada, "Self and Language in the Fall," V, 213–28.

Dan S. Collins, "The Buoyant Mind in Milton's Eden," V, 229–48.

Charlotte F. Otten, " 'My Native Element': Milton's Paradise and English Gardens," V, 249–67.

Barbara K. Lewalski, "Milton on Women—Yet Once More," VI, 3–20.

Leonora Leet Brodwin, "Milton and the Renaissance Circe," VI, 21–83.

Anne B. Long, " 'She May Have More Shapes than One': Milton and the Modern Idea That Truth Changes," VI, 85–99.

Virginia R. Mollenkott, "Milton's Technique of Multiple Choice," VI, 101–11.

Dustin H. Griffin, "Milton's Evening," VI, 259–76.

Peter Lindenbaum, "Lovemaking in Milton's Paradise," VI, 277–306.

B. Rajan, "The Cunning Resemblance," VII, 29–48.

Ernst Häublein, "Milton's Paraphrase of Genesis: A Stylistic Reading of *Paradise Lost*, Book VII," VII, 101–25.

Jason P. Rosenblatt, "The Mosaic Voice in *Paradise Lost*," VII, 207–32.

Michael Lieb, "*Paradise Lost* and the Myth of Prohibition," VII, 233–65.

Albert C. Labriola, "The Aesthetics of Self-Diminution: Christian Iconography and *Paradise Lost*," VII, 267–311.

G. Stanley Koehler, "Milton and the Art of Landscape," VIII, 3–40.

Leonora Leet Brodwin, "The Dissolution of Satan in *Paradise Lost*: A Study of Milton's Heretical Eschatology," VIII, 165–207.

John T. Shawcross, "The Rhetor as Creator in *Paradise Lost*," VIII, 209–19.

Nicholas R. Jones, " 'Stand' and 'Fall' as Images of Posture in *Paradise Lost*," VIII, 221–46.

Beverley Sherry, "Speech in *Paradise Lost*," VIII, 247–66.

Desmond M. Hamlet, "Recalcitrance, Damnation, and the Justice of God in *Paradise Lost*," VIII, 267–91.

Marcia Landy, " 'A Free and Open Encounter': Milton and the Modern Reader," IX, 3–36.

Don Parry Norford, "The Sacred Head: Milton's Solar Mysticism," IX, 37–75.

Burton J. Weber, "The Non-Narrative Approaches to *Paradise Lost*: A Gentle Remonstrance," IX, 77–103.

Harold E. Toliver, "Milton's Household Epic," IX, 105–20.

Kathleen M. Swaim, " 'Hee for God Only, Shee for God in Him': Structural Parallelism in *Paradise Lost*," IX, 121–49.

Dustin Griffin, "Milton's Moon," IX, 151–67.

E. R. Gregory, "Three Muses and a Poet: A Perspective on Milton's Epic Thought," X, 35–64.

Mark Crispin Miller, "Beelzebub and Adam and 'the worst that can be,' " X, 65–76.

George Yost, "A New Look at Milton's Paradise," X, 77–91.

Robert L. Entzminger, "Epistemology and the Tutelary Word in *Paradise Lost*," X, 93–109.

Stephen Wigler, "Outrageous Noise and the Sovereign Voice: Satan, Sin, and Syntax in *Sonnet XIX* and Book VI of *Paradise Lost*," X, 155–65.

Don Parry Norford, "The Separation of the World Parents in *Paradise Lost*," XII, 3–24.

Diane McColley, "Eve's Dream," XII, 25–45.

Dennis Danielson, "Milton's Arminianism and *Paradise Lost*," XII, 47–73.

Douglas A. Northrop, "The Double Structure of *Paradise Lost*," XII, 75–90.

Paradise Regained

Jackson I. Cope, "*Paradise Regained:* Inner Ritual," I, 51–65.

Roger H. Sundell, "The Narrator as Interpreter in *Paradise Regained*," II, 83–101.

James R. McAdams, "The Pattern of Temptation in *Paradise Regained*," IV, 177–93.

Lee M. Johnson, "Milton's Blank Verse Sonnets," V, 129–53.

Leonora Leet Brodwin, "Milton and the Renaissance Circe," VI, 21–83.

Elaine B. Safer, "The Socratic Dialogue and 'Knowledge in the Making' in *Paradise Regained*," VI, 215–26.

Emory Elliott, "Milton's Biblical Style in *Paradise Regained*," VI, 227–41.

B. Rajan, "The Cunning Resemblance," VII, 29–48.

A. B. Chambers, "The Double Time Scheme in *Paradise Regained*," VII, 189–205.

Richard Douglas Jordan, "*Paradise Regained* and the Second Adam," IX, 261–75.

David Renaker, "The Horoscope of Christ," XII, 213–33.

Malcolm Kelsall, "The Historicity of *Paradise Regained*," XII, 235–51.

Edward Le Comte, "Satan's Heresies in *Paradise Regained*," XII, 253–66.

Ad Patrem

John Spencer Hill, "Poet-Priest: Vocational Tension in Milton's Early Development," VIII, 41–69.

Prolusion 7

Leonora Leet Brodwin, "Milton and the Renaissance Circe," VI, 21–83.

In Quintum Novembris

Stella P. Revard, "Milton's Gunpowder Poems and Satan's Conspiracy," IV, 63–77.

The Readie and Easie Way

Keith W. Stavely, "The Style and Structure of Milton's *Readie and Easie Way*," V, 269–87.

The Reason of Church-Government

Michael Lieb, "Milton and the Organicist Polemic," IX, 79–99.
John A. Via, "Milton's Antiprelatical Tracts: The Poet Speaks in Prose," V, 87–127.
Annabel Patterson, "The Civic Hero in Milton's Prose," VIII, 71–101.

Of Reformation

Michael Lieb, "Milton and the Organicist Polemic," IV, 79–99.
John A. Via, "Milton's Antiprelatical Tracts: The Poet Speaks in Prose," V, 87–127.
Annabel Patterson, "The Civic Hero in Milton's Prose," VIII, 71–101.

Rhetoric

John M. Steadman, "Milton's Rhetoric: Satan and the 'Unjust Discourse,'" I, 67–92.
D. M. Rosenberg, "Parody of Style in Milton's Polemics," II, 113–18.
James Egan, "Milton and the Marprelate Tradition," VIII, 103–21.
Irene Samuel, "Milton on the Province of Rhetoric," X, 177–93.
John M. Perlette, "Milton, Ascham, and the Rhetoric of the Divorce Controversy," X, 195–215.

Samson Agonistes

Louis L. Martz, "Chorus and Character in *Samson Agonistes*," I, 115–34.
John S. Hill, "Vocation and Spiritual Renovation in *Samson Agonistes*," II, 149–74.
Marcia Landy, "Language and the Seal of Silence in *Samson Agonistes*," II, 175–94.
Nancy Y. Hoffman, "Samson's Other Father: The Character of Manoa in *Samson Agonistes*," II, 195–210.

Sherman H. Hawkins, "Samson's Catharsis," II, 211–30.

Samuel S. Stollman, "Milton's Samson and the Jewish Tradition," III, 185–200.

Jackie Di Salvo, " 'The Lord's Battells': *Samson Agonistes* and the Puritan Revolution," IV, 39–62.

John C. Ulreich, Jr., "The Typological Structure of Milton's Imagery," V, 67–85.

Lee M. Johnson, "Milton's Blank Verse Sonnets," V, 129–53.

Leonora Leet Brodwin, "Milton and the Renaissance Circe," VI, 21–83.

Carole S. Kessner, "Milton's Hebraic Herculean Hero," VI, 243–58.

B. Rajan, "The Cunning Resemblance," VII, 29–48.

Christopher Grose, " 'His Uncontrollable Intent': Discovery as Action in *Samson Agonistes*," VII, 49–76.

Marcia Landy, " 'A Free and Open Encounter': Milton and the Modern Reader," IX, 3–36.

Don Parry Norford, "The Sacred Head: Milton's Solar Mysticism," IX, 37–75.

C. A. Patrides, "The Comic Dimension in Greek Tragedy and *Samson Agonistes*," X, 3–21.

John B. Mason, "Multiple Perspectives in *Samson Agonistes:* Critical Attitudes Toward Dalila," X, 23–33.

Helen Damico, "Duality in Dramatic Vision: A Structural Analysis of *Samson Agonistes*," XII, 91–116.

John N. Wall, Jr., "The Contrarious Hand of God: *Samson Agonistes* and the Biblical Lament," XII, 117–39.

Joan S. Bennett, "Liberty Under the Law: The Chorus and the Meaning of *Samson Agonistes*," XII, 141–63.

Sonnet 7

John Spencer Hill, "Poet-Priest: Vocational Tension in Milton's Early Development," VIII, 41–69.

Sonnet 18

Nicholas R. Jones, "The Education of the Faithful in Milton's Piedmontese Sonnet," X, 167–76.

Sonnet 19

Gary A. Stringer, "Milton's 'Thorn in the Flesh': Pauline Didacticism in *Sonnet XIX*," X, 141–54.

Stephen Wigler, "Outrageous Noise and the Sovereign Voice: Satan, Sin, and Syntax in *Sonnet XIX* and Book VI of *Paradise Lost*," X, 155–65.

Sonnet 23

Marilyn L. Williamson, "A Reading of Milton's Twenty-Third Sonnet," IV, 141–49.

John C. Ulreich, Jr., "The Typological Structure of Milton's Imagery," V, 67–85.

John J. Colaccio, " 'A Death like Sleep': The Christology of Milton's Twenty-Third Sonnet," VI, 181–97.

Dixon Fiske, "The Theme of Purification in Milton's *Sonnet XXIII*," VII, 149–63.

Kurt Heinzelman, " 'Cold Consolation': The Art of Milton's Last Sonnet," X, 111–25.

John Spencer Hill, " 'Alcestis from the Grave': Image and Structure in *Sonnet XXIII*," X, 127–39.

Typology

John C. Ulreich, Jr., "The Typological Structure of Milton's Imagery," V, 67–85.

Jonathan Goldberg, "*Virga Iesse:* Analogy, Typology, and Anagogy in a Miltonic Simile," V, 177–90.

John J. Colaccio, " 'A Death like Sleep': The Christology of Milton's Twenty-Third Sonnet," VI, 181–97.

Jason P. Rosenblatt, "The Mosaic Voice in *Paradise Lost*," VII, 207–32.

Albert C. Labriola, "The Aesthetics of Self-Diminution: Christian Iconography and *Paradise Lost*," VII, 267–311.

Richard Douglas Jordan, "*Paradise Regained* and the Second Adam," IX, 261–75.

Women

Marcia Landy, "Kinship and the Role of Women in *Paradise Lost*," IV, 3–18.

Barbara K. Lewalski, "Milton on Women—Yet Once More," VI, 3–20.

Marcia Landy, " 'A Free and Open Encounter': Milton and the Modern Reader," IX, 3–36.

INDEX

Abdiel, IV, 28, 29; IX, 8–9
  as epic hero, II, 212
  intellect of, VI, 14
  and Louvet, XI, 89–90
  and Milton, VIII, 49
  posture of, VIII, 238–39
  in War in Heaven, III, 172, 178–
    80
Aboth de Rabbi Nathan, VII, 241
Abraham, III, 164, 165, 167; IX,
  126
Abrams, M. H., on *Lycidas,* IV, 152
Accidence Commenced Grammar, X,
  181
Accommodation
  in Augustinian epistemology, X,
    94
  defined, VI, 89
  in *De Doctrina Christiana,* VI, 86,
    91–93
  in *PL,* I, 23–24, 151, 155; III,
    160; VI, 93–97; VIII, 210, 212,
    271; X, 103
  in *SA,* VI, 97
Action and contemplation
  in *L'Allegro* and *Il Penseroso,* IX,
    209–18
  in Milton's prose, VIII, 72–75, 78–
    84, 86, 89, 90, 92–94
  in *PL,* I, 36, 44
  in *PR,* IX, 273
  in Puritanism, IV, 43, 44–45, 55–
    56
  in *SA,* IV, 44–45

  in Tasso, III, 84–85, 86, 89–91,
    92–94, 96, 98, 100; VIII, 74–75.
    See also Contemplation; Wisdom
    and strength
Acts of the Apostles
  Moses in, VII, 224–25
  as source for *Areopagitica,* IV,
    102, 111–12
  as source for Blake's *Milton,* XI,
    56–60
  as source for *PL,* VII, 211
  as source for *PR,* VI, 235, 236;
    VII, 195
  as source for *Sonnet 19,* X, 144–
    45, 146
Adam
  and Aeneas, I, 32
  antifeminism of, IV, 14–15
  and Beelzebub, X, 68, 70–73
  and Christ, VII, 268–69, 273, 287,
    304–05; IX, 261–63, 265–66,
    268–69, 271
  creation of, V, 239–40; VII, 270–
    77
  curiosity of, IX, 131–34
  dream of, X, 82–83
  education of, I, 45, 148; II, 53,
    54; V, 140–42, 241–43; VI,
    301; X, 95–100, 102–03
  fall of, V, 220–23; VI, 298; VIII,
    240–41; IX, 87; X, 101–03;
    XII, 6, 83–84
  as father, IV, 8; IX, 17–18
  humility of, X, 74–75

15

Adam *(cont.)*
  language of, IV, 8; VIII, 253–54,
    256–57; X, 104–06
  and Manoa, II, 209
  pride of, V, 12–13
  in rabbinical tradition, XII, 17
  and St. Michael, I, 45
  and Samson, II, 219–20, 227, 228;
    VII, 59
  and Satan, I, 103–07; X, 73–74;
    XII, 86
  self-knowledge of, III, 107; V,
    160–61; X, 95–96
  soliloquies of, V, 220–21, 222;
    VII, 52–53; IX, 145; X, 70–75
  sonnet of, V, 140–42
  temptation of, V, 19–20; VI, 290–
    91.
  See also Adam and Eve
Adam and Eve
  diction of, compared, IX, 129–30,
    132
  hospitality of, I, 135–37, 139–40,
    141–42
  interdependence of, VI, 6–8, 17–
    19; VII, 273–78, 283–87, 290–
    92, 295
  not tragic figures, V, 11–21
  as parents, VI, 9
  prayers of, I, 179; V, 169–70, 237;
    VIII, 252; IX, 141–43
  as reflections of God, IV, 33–35
  and Satan, I, 103–07
  as sculpture, VIII, 30–31
  sexuality of, I, 162–64; VI, 6,
    265
  as siblings, IV, 6–7
  and Sin and Death, VII, 289
  as "world parents," XII, 5–6.
  See also Adam; Eve
Adamson, J. H., on *PL,* IX, 53–54,
  61
Adamson, J. W., on education, IX,
  204

Addison, Joseph
  Arnold on, XI, 110
  on *PL,* V, 80; IX, 128, 152
"Adhere," VII, 275–76
Ad Herennium, XII, 202
Adiaphorism, IV, 88
Adolescence, in *Comus,* VI, 169–72,
  174–77
Ad Patrem. See under *Patrem*
Advent, VI, 136*n*4
Aeschylus, tragicomedy of, X, 7–8
Agape, VI, 184
Agar, Herbert, on *PR,* VI, 216
Aggadic Midrash, Samson in, VI,
  247
"Agonistes," II, 183–84; IV, 41, 44–
  45; VII, 57
Agricola, IV, 127, 128–29, 131,
  132–36
D'Ailly, Pierre, XII, 222–23
Ainsworth, Henry, VII, 276; XII, 32,
  34
Aion, defined, XII, 197
Air, in Paradise, II, 41; V, 157–58,
  251–52, 255–57
Airs, Lydian, in *L'Allegro,* VII, 86–
  87; IX, 217. *See also* Music
Albertus Magnus, IX, 59; XII, 220–
  22
  —*Speculum Astronomiae,* XII,
    221
Albumasar
  —*Greater Introduction to
    Astronomy,* XII, 221
Alcestis
  in Chaucer, X, 130–32
  and Christ, VI, 184
  Neoplatonic view of, VIII, 156–
    57; X, 131–32
  in Plato, X, 130
  in *Sonnet 23,* IV, 143, 147–48; V,
    76–77; VI, 182, 184–85; VIII,
    153, 156–58; X, 111–12, 116–
    22, 127–39

Alchemy, II, 19, 21; IX, 52–53, 57, 58–60, 62, 68; XII, 20–21

Allegory
in *Animadversions*, VIII, 112
in Milton's early poetry, V, 120
in *PL*, V, 79–80 (*see also* Death; Sin)
in *PR*, VI, 223
and personification, distinguished, V, 74

L'Allegro
ambiguity in, VII, 81–82, 96
dawn in, VII, 79–80, 81
epithalamic motifs in, V, 41
imagery of, VIII, 13
landscape in, VII, 85; VIII, 10, 11, 12, 13
lark in, V, 74; VII, 78, 81; VIII, 134
Lydian airs in, VII, 86–87; IX, 217
Orpheus in, VII, 86, 93; IX, 215
pastoral in, VII, 85
reading of, VII, 77–87
trees in, VIII, 15–16
unity of, VII, 87.
See also *L'Allegro* and *Il Penseroso*

L'Allegro, VII, 78, 81, 95

L'Allegro and *Il Penseroso*
action and contemplation in, IX, 209–18
and *An Apology*, V, 110
Blake's illustrations for, VIII, 123–47
and chivalric tales, IX, 212–13
Circe in, VI, 43–46
color in, III, 58, 59, 70
contrasted, VII, 87–95; VIII, 126–28
cyclical nature of, VI, 43–46
education in, IX, 209–18
and *Elegy 1*, VI, 43
Homer's influence in, IX, 210
imagery of, IX, 212

Mirth and Melancholy in, III, 58; VII, 78, 81, 95; IX, 209–18
nature in, IX, 212
Philomel in, V, 74
poet in, IX, 106
and Pope's *Eloisa to Abelard*, XI, 33
regeneracy in, V, 103, 107, 112
water in, VIII, 13.
See also *L'Allegro; Il Penseroso*

Allen, D. C.
on *L'Allegro* and *Il Penseroso*, VII, 83, 90, 91, 97–98; VIII, 56, 126–28, 140; IX, 214
on Dalila, X, 26, 28
on *Lycidas*, III, 63; IX, 224–25
on pagan symbolism, IV, 173
on *PL*, III, 70–71; VII, 208–09
on *PR*, XII, 255
on *Prolusion 3*, IX, 206
on *Sonnet 23*, X, 129

Allestree, Richard
—*The Government of the Tongue*, VIII, 249–50, 252, 257, 259

Alliteration, in *PL*, III, 148–50; IV, 27

Alpheus, in *Lycidas*, III, 15, 50

Alpheus and Arethusa, IX, 225, 232

Ambiguity
in *L'Allegro*, VII, 81–82, 96
in *Lycidas*, II, 119–20, 124, 126–27
as Miltonic technique, VI, 101–11
in *PL*, II, 27, 28; VIII, 166–76, 181; XII, 20
in *Il Penseroso*, VII, 88–89
in *SA*, II, 201
about theology, in Milton, VI, 102–05

Ambivalence
of Christianity, II, 104, 106–07, 109
in *PL*, I, 47–48
in Virgil, I, 46–48

Ambrose, St., V, 168
  hymns of, VII, 174
Ames, Ruth, on Moses, IX, 228
Ames, William
  —*Medvlla S. S. Theologiae*, IX,
    253–54
Amyot, Jacques, on history, X, 40
Anabaptism, VI, 48–49; VIII, 193–
  202
Anadiplosis, in *PL*, III, 141–42
Analogy, V, 178–79, 181–82, 187
  in *Doctrine and Discipline of
    Divorce*, X, 205–07, 208
  in *PL*, II, 61
  in *Sonnet 23*, IV, 142–44
Anaphora, in *PL*, III, 146–47
Anaxagoras, IX, 54
Andreini, Giambattista
  —*L'Adamo*, II, 46–47
Andrewes, Lancelot, IV, 64, 65;
  VII, 192, 193
Angels
  faithful, I, 107–09 (*see also*
    Abdiel; Michael, St.; Raphael)
  fallen, I, 85–88, 109–10; II, 77–
    78; VI, 107, 108–09; VII, 252–
    53, 296; VIII, 284–85; IX, 82–
    83 (*see also* Beelzebub; Belial;
    Satan)
  knowledge of evil of, III, 128–30
  love among, VI, 296–97
  in Revelation, XI, 52, 53, 54, 56,
    57, 60–62, 66, 70, 72–73
Animadversions
  allegory in, VIII, 112
  and *Comus*, V, 96, 97
  gardening in, V, 252
  heroism in, VIII, 78–79, 83
  imagery of, V, 91, 92, 105–06;
    VIII, 112–13
  light in, V, 111; VIII, 113
  and *Lycidas*, V, 98–99, 100
  Marprelate influence in, VIII,
    108–13

Moses in, VII, 213
  and Nativity ode, V, 106
  occasion of, VIII, 108
  parody in, II, 117–18
  poetic destiny in, VIII, 66
  prayer in, VIII, 111–12
  priesthood in, III, 24–25
  and *In Quintum Novembris*, V,
    92, 93
  Ramism in, VI, 208; X, 181
  regeneracy in, V, 105–06, 107–08,
    109, 111
  Revelation in, VI, 114–15; VIII,
    112–13
  satire in, V, 89–90; VIII, 108–13
  scatology in, II, 116
  worship in, I, 171, 179
Animals, in *PL* and *PR*, VIII, 26.
  See also Imagery, animal
Animism, in *PL*, VII, 250–51
Annunciation
  iconography of, VII, 300–02
  and temptation of Eve, VII, 300
Antichrist legend, VI, 115–17, 119,
  121, 128–30, 133–34, 137n11
  in *Areopagitica*, IV, 105
  in Chester plays, VI, 134–35
  in *Christus Triumphans*, VI, 126,
    129
  in *Comus*, VI, 129, 132
  in *De Doctrina Christiana*, VI, 130
  English reformers on, VI, 130
Anticipation, in *PL*, I, 11–12
Antiepiscopal pamphlets. *See* Anti-
  prelatical tracts
Antifeminism
  Adam's, IV, 14–15
  of Chorus (*SA*), I, 129–30
  medieval, V, 56
  Milton's, IV, 4–5.
  See also Women
Antihero, VII, 128–29. *See also*
  Satan, false heroism of
Antimonarchical pamphlets, Tacitus'

influence in, IV, 123–25. *See also*
*Eikonoklastes; Tenure of Kings
and Magistrates*
Antiprelatical tracts
authority in, I, 17–20
autobiographical elements in, V,
112–21, 124–25
church in, VI, 122
as development of earlier works,
V, 87–127
imagery of, I, 18–19; V, 91–94
law in, XII, 142
liberty in, XII, 142
light in, V, 100
Milton's vocational choice in, VIII,
55, 65
organicism in, IV, 79–99
pastoral in, V, 99–100, 109, 110,
120
regeneracy in, V, 87–127
and *Second Defence,* V, 90
Tacitus' influence in, IV, 122–23.
See also *Animadversions;
An Apology for Smectymnuus;
Of Prelatical Episcopacy; The
Reason of Church-Government;
Of Reformation*
Antitraditionalism, in Milton, I, 21;
IV, 109; X, 184–87. *See also*
Tradition
Apocalypse
in Nativity ode, IV, 170–71
in *PL,* VIII, 172–76
Apocalyptic plays. *See* Mystery
plays
Apocatastasis, XII, 260
Apocrypha, VII, 214
Apollinarian heresy, XII, 259
Apollo, in *Lycidas,* III, 37
An Apology for Smectymnuus
and *L'Allegro* and *Il Penseroso,* V,
110
and *Arcades,* V, 110, 111
Arminianism in, XII, 60

authority in, X, 184
autobiographical elements in, VI,
41–42
biblical sources of, V, 99–100
ceremony in, VIII, 154
chastity in, V, 118-19, 121; VI,
42; VIII, 83
Christ in, VII, 60
Circe in, VI, 41–43, 54
and *Comus,* V, 96, 110, 111, 118
education in, V, 117–18
God in, V, 111–12
heroism in, VII, 82–84
history in, II, 138
imagery of, V, 90, 91, 106, 110–
11, 116–17
irony in, V, 117
light in, V, 110–11
and *Lycidas,* V, 99–100, 110, 119
and Milton's early poetry, V, 106,
110–12, 119
Moses in, VII, 226
occasion of, V, 116–17
opposing truths in, VI, 91
parody in, II, 117–18
and *Ad Patrem,* V, 110
personal statement in, IV, 112–13,
116–21
rabbinical sources of, IV, 196–97
regeneracy in, V, 106, 108, 110–
12
rhetoric of, X, 183
scatology in, II, 116
wisdom and strength in, VII,
50–52
Apotheosis
of Diodati, VII, 127–28, 129–30
of Milton, XI, 66–68
Apotheosis tradition, XI, 66–68
"Apparent," in *PL,* IX, 161
Aquinas, St. Thomas
on delight, VI, 190
on intellect, VI, 188
on resurrection, VIII, 195–96

Aquinas, St. Thomas (cont.)
  on self-delusion, X, 116
  —Summa Theologica, V, 173
Arbiter, in PL, VI, 270–71
Arcades
  allegory in, V, 120
  and An Apology, V, 110, 111
  color in, III, 69
  imagery of, V, 93–94, 122
  muses in, X, 38
  music in, VI, 45
  pastoral in, V, 120
  performance of, III, 218; V, 4
  and The Reason of Church-
    Government, V, 93–94
  and Of Reformation, V, 94, 104,
    109
  regeneracy in, V, 107, 112, 120,
    124
Arcadia, II, 45–47
Arcana imperii, IV, 118, 121, 131
Areopagitica, V, 270; XII, 261
  Antichrist in, IV, 105
  Arminianism in, XII, 60
  biblical sources of, IV, 102, 111–
    12; IX, 198, 199
  book metaphor in, IX, 190–93,
    194
  church in, I, 150
  contraries in, VII, 36–37
  Cupid in, VII, 36–37
  education in, VI, 220, 221
  and Eliot's Little Gidding, XI, 121
  and Euripides, IV, 112
  evil in, III, 125; V, 8; XII, 37
  exordium of, IV, 102–03, 104
  Fall of Man in, XII, 28
  heroism in, VIII, 85–87
  history in, IX, 173–74, 176
  imagery of, VII, 36–37; IX, 169–
    70, 179–82, 185–201
  irony in, IV, 104–05, 109–11, 112
  and Isocrates, IV, 101–15
  knowledge in, III, 132–33

liberty in, IV, 105–06, 108
mind in, V, 231
Moses in, VII, 211–12, 219
nationalism in, IX, 189
occasion of, IX, 187–88
organicism in, IV, 97
organization of, IX, 171–73, 174–
  79
Parliament in, IX, 189–90
parody in, II, 115; VII, 36–37
phoenix in, IX, 198
St. Paul in, IV, 111–12
Samson in, IV, 39–40; VI, 246;
  IX, 49
sarcasm in, IX, 173–74
sin in, III, 130
Spirit in, I, 150
style of, IV, 108–09; IX, 169–84
symmetry in, IV, 177
syntax of, IX, 170–71, 174
title of, IV, 101–02, 104, 111,
  112, 113; IX, 188
Tree of Knowledge in, IX, 115–16
truth in, IV, 97; VI, 90–91; VII,
  36–37; VIII, 86; IX, 6, 179–82,
  183, 196–97
"warfaring Christian" in, VIII,
  100n22; IX, 197–98
wisdom and strength in, IX, 185–
  201
worship in, I, 183
Areté, VI, 244, 250, 254
Arianism, XII, 257
Ariel, in PL, IV, 210–13
Ariosto
  Circe in, VI, 26–28
  muse of, III, 27
  —Orlando Furioso, I, 46; II, 62–
    63; III, 27; VI, 26–28; X, 59–
    60
Aristophanes
  on rhetoric, I, 68–69
  —Clouds, I, 68–69
  —The Frogs, X, 14

Aristotle
  on *agon*, IV, 44
  on brutishness, VI, 57, 79n32,
    82n54
  on character, I, 72–73
  in *Of Education*, V, 8
  on Plato's dialogues, VI, 216–17
  on rhetoric, X, 180, 181, 184,
    187, 202, 203
  on tragedy, I, 70; V, 6, 7, 8
  —*Nicomachean Ethics*, VIII, 72,
    79–80
  —*Poetics*, I, 45–46, 69, 70, 72–73;
    II, 216; III, 122; V, 8–9; X, 3,
    4, 8, 9
  —*Rhetoric*, II, 135; X, 180, 181,
    184, 187, 202, 203
Arminianism
  defined, XII, 47–48
  free will and grace in, XII, 56–59
  history of, XII, 55–56
  in Milton, XII, 60, 61, 62–70
  Milton on, XII, 48, 60–61
  motives of, XII, 59
Arminius, Jacobus, XII, 55
Arms and letters *topos*, VIII, 74
Arnold, Matthew
  career of, XI, 105–06
  and Milton, XI, 99, 105–13
  on *PL*, XI, 108–13
  on *PR*, XI, 111
  on Wordsworth, XI, 113
  —*Essays in Criticism*, XI, 113
  —"A French Critic on Milton,"
    XI, 109–12
  —"Maurice de Guérin," XI, 110
  —"The Study of Poetry," XI,
    112–13
  —"On Translating Homer," XI,
    109
Arrowsmith, William, on Heracles,
  VI, 245, 250–51, 254
Art
  and nature, V, 259

in Paradise, VIII, 29–32
Arthuriad, planned by Milton, II,
  141; VIII, 64, 71–72, 76; X, 45
Artis Logicae. See *Art of Logic*
Art of Logic, VI, 207; VII, ix, 247;
  VIII, 249; IX, 244–45, 246, 250;
  X, 55, 57, 180–81, 183, 187; XII,
  215, 222
Ascalon, XII, 98
Ascham, Anthony, X, 195–96; XII,
  171
  —*Discourse*, X, 211–12
  —"Of Marriage," X, 195, 196–
    204, 210–11
Ascham, Roger
  —*The Scholemaster*, VI, 131
Ashe, Simeon, IV, 51
Ashtaroth, in Nativity ode, IV, 172–
  73; IX, 158
Assumption of Moses, VIII, 188
Astrology
  Calvin on, XII, 225
  in *De Doctrina Christiana*, XII,
    216–17
  in *Epitaphium Damonis*, XII, 214
  Kepler on, XII, 216
  Luther on, XII, 225
  in *Lycidas*, XII, 214
  in Middle Ages, XII, 220–25
  in Nativity ode, XII, 214, 223
  natural and judicial, XII, 214–16
  in *PL*, XII, 214–15
  in *PR*, XII, 213–14, 231
  patristic view of, XII, 218–20
  in *Il Penseroso*, XII, 214
  in *Second Defence*, XII, 214
At a Solemn Musick. See under
  Solemn
At a Vacation Exercise. See under
  Vacation
Atropos, in *Lycidas*, II, 124–25, 126
Attendant Spirit (*Comus*)
  as daemon, VI, 81n50, 132–33
  diction of, VI, 151–52

Attendant Spirit *(cont.)*
  and landscape, VI, 146–48
  as Orpheus figure, IX, 43–44
  sincerity of, VI, 150
  as teacher, V, 298–99, 303
  virtue and skill of, V, 290, 292–93
Attersoll, William, on Moses, VII,
  212–13
Aubrey, John, V, 252; XI, 7, 8
Audley, Elizabeth, III, 202, 203,
  205, 212, 213, 215, 216, 217
Audley, James, III, 212, 214
Augustine, St.
  on the cross, VII, 281
  on day and night, IX, 80
  epistemology of, X, 94
  on evil, VIII, 283–84
  on Fall of Man, V, 197
  on free will and grace, XII, 50–
  52, 68
  on Genesis, VII, 269
  on glory, X, 52
  on the magi, XII, 220
  on magic, X, 105
  on metaphor, X, 103–04
  on Moses, VII, 210, 224
  on rule of charity, VI, 201–02
  on sexual intercourse, VI, 279–81
  on Tree of Knowledge, VII, 248
  on withdrawal from world, XII,
  31–32
  —*The City of God,* VI, 279–81;
  XII, 50–51
  —*Confessions,* VI, 201
  —*De Doctrina Christiana,* VI, 202
  —*De Genesi ad Litteram,* VI, 280
  —*On Grace and Free Will,* XII,
  51–52
  —*On Merits and Forgiveness of
  Sins,* VII, 248
  —*Sermo Suppositus,* VII, 281, 290
Augustus, XII, 242–43
Ausonius, XII, 202, 205
Austen, Ralph, V, 255, 257, 258, 262

Authority
  of Bible, I, 148–149; VIII, 118;
  X, 186–87
  divine and human, IX, 9–10
  God's, IV, 23–25
  Milton on, I, 17–21
  Milton's rhetorical use of, X, 183–
  87
  in *PL,* IV, 8, 13, 14–16, 17, 20–25
  and Puritan revolution, IV, 46
  St. Paul on, IV, 23.
  See also Tradition
Avarice, in *PR,* IV, 183, 186–88
"Avenge, O Lord, thy slaughter'd
  Saints." See *Sonnet 18*
Avitus
  —*Poematum de Mosaicae
  historiae . . . ,* V, 48
Aylmer, G. E., XII, 182
Azazel, in *PL,* IV, 213–14

Baalim, IV, 172–73
Babb, Lawrence, on *PL,* V, 253–54
Babel, Tower of, VIII, 249; X,
  84–87
Babington, Gervase
  —*Comfortable Notes Vpon the
  bookes of Exodus and Leuiticus,*
  VII, 256
Babylon, II, 8; X, 81–84
Babylonian Talmud, VI, 247; VII,
  256
Bacchus legend, in *Comus,* VI, 131–
  32
Bachelard, Gaston, IX, 51–52, 55
Bachofen, J. J., IX, 40–41
Bacon, Francis
  on landscape, II, 45; VIII, 6–7,
  12, 16
  methodology of, X, 101
  —"Of Gardens," V, 252, 254, 259,
  261; VIII, 6–7, 12, 16
Baker, Stewart A., *III, 35–53*
  on *Lycidas,* IX, 222

Balance, in *PL*, VI, 270
Bale, John, IX, 273
—*Image of Bothe Churches*, VI, 117–18, 120
—*The Pageant of Popes*, VI, 131
Banks, Theodore
on *Areopagitica*, IX, 185
on Milton's military imagery, IV, 59
Baptism, XII, 254–55
of Christ, II, 85–87; IX, 267
in Tasso, III, 95
Barbelognostics, XII, 18
Barber, C. L., on Marprelate, VIII, 106
Barfield, Owen, V, 73, 74
Barker, Arthur E.
on *Areopagitica*, VI, 90
on *Comus*, V, 94
on *Lycidas*, VIII, 48, 53
on Nativity ode, II, 105; VII, 177–78
on *PL*, XII, 75, 77
on *SA*, II, 149; III, 197; XII, 141, 142
on truth, VI, 92–93
Barlaeus, Caspar, V, 51, 53, 54, 55, 57–58
Barlow, William, IV, 64
Baroque
in landscape, VIII, 11–12, 16–19, 21, 27
in prose, V, 274
Baroway, Israel, VII, 212
Barran, Henry de
—*Tragique Comedy Francoise de l'homme iustifié par Foy*, V, 20
Barrow, Isaac, IV, 65
Bartas, Guillaume de Salluste du
Eden of, II, 45
on sexual intercourse, VI, 282, 283
—"The commodities of Mariage," V, 57

—*Devine Weekes and Workes*, V, 57; IX, 231; X, 58
—"Epithalamie," V, 55–56
—*Urania*, X, 56
Baruch, Franklin R., V, *289–308*
Barzun, Jacques, XII, 191
Basil, St., I, 152–53
Battle
in Nativity ode, IV, 170–71
as spiritual metaphor, IV, 47–50
verbal, I, 89–90.
See also Imagery, military; War in Heaven
Baxter, Nathaniel, V, 54
Baxter, Richard, IV, 50; XII, 27
—*The Christians Converse with God*, VIII, 262–63
Bayne, Ronald, on *Comus*, VI, 144
Beaumont, Joseph, II, 44
Becon, Thomas, IX, 267
Beelzebub, I, 56; III, 179; IV, 68, 69; VII, 159n5; VIII, 179–80; X, 65–70
and Adam, X, 68, 70–73
Satan's speeches to, I, 81–84
Behrendt, Stephen C., *VIII, 123–47*
Belial, I, 35; IV, 74; V, 302
as Circean tempter, IV, 136, 137; VI, 59, 65–66
on death, VIII, 178, 182
as father of Antichrist, VI, 128
and Manoa, II, 202
name of, I, 182
rhetoric of, I, 70
Bell, Millicent, on *PL*, III, 120, 121; IX, 89, 92; XII, 6, 7
Bellerophon, as type of Satan, II, 69
Ben Gerson, Rabbi Levi, III, 187, 188–89; IV, 199–200, 202–05, 211
Ben Isaac, Rabbi Solomon. *See* Rashi
Benjamin, Edwin B., *IV, 117–40*
Bennett, Joan S., *XII, 141–63*
Bentley, Richard, II, 31; XI, 31
Berchorius, VII, 14

Berkeley, David S., on *Lycidas*, IX, 222, 224

Bernard, Richard
—"Bible Battells," IV, 47, 48
—*The Isle of Man*, IV, 80

Bernard of Clairvaux, VI, 124–25; XII, 32

Bespaloff, Rachel, on Homer, X, 6

Best, Paul
—*Mysteries Discovered*, VIII, 197

Bethell, Slingsley, IV, 43

Bible
as authority, I, 148–49; VIII, 118; X, 186–88
Authorized Version of, VII, 102, 107–09, 110, 112–15, 116–20; XII, 128
in *De Doctrina Christiana*, XII, 48
gardens in, V, 251
as history, XII, 238–39, 250
in *The History of Britain*, XII, 238
illustration of, VII, 272–73, 300, 301
imprecision of, as treated by Milton, VI, 103–04
interpretation of, VI, 229–30
Milton's use of, XII, 30
myth of exodus in, II, 6–7, 8
versions of, known by Milton, VII, 102.
See also Acts of the Apostles; Apocrypha; Daniel, Book of; Deuteronomy; Exodus, Book of; Ezekiel, Book of; Genesis, Book of; Geneva Bible; Haggai; Isaiah, Book of; James, Epistle of; Jeremiah; Job, Book of; Joel; John, St., Gospel of; John the Divine, St., Revelation of; Jude, General Epistle of; Judges, Book of; Kings, First Book of; Lamentations of Jeremiah; Leviticus, Book of; Luke, St., Gospel of; Malachi; Mark, St., Gospel of; Matthew, St., Gospel of; Numbers, Book of; Paul, St.; Peter, St.; Proverbs; Psalms; Samuel, Book of; Song of Solomon; Zechariah

Biblia Pauperum, VII, 273, 274, 294, 298–99

Biblical lament
defined, XII, 120
described, XII, 126
in *SA*, XII, 127–37
tone of, XII, 127

Biddle, John
—*Twofold Catechism*, VIII, 198

"Bishop," in *Of Reformation*, X, 189–90

Bishops' Wars, VIII, 54

Blackburn, Thomas H., III, 119–37; V, 191–211

Blackmore, Sir Richard
—*Prince Arthur*, I, 54

Blaeu, Johan
—*Le Grand Atlas*, X, 79

Blake, William
illustrations for *L'Allegro* and *Il Penseroso* by, VIII, 123–47
on imagination, VIII, 137
and Milton, XI, viii–ix, 51–82
on *PL*, II, 60; IX, 89
—*A Descriptive Catalogue*, XI, 66, 76
—*Jerusalem*, XI, 76
—*The Marriage of Heaven and Hell*, VIII, 128; XI, 76
—*Milton*, VII, 219; VIII, 126; XI, 51; XII, 19
—*Songs of Innocence and of Experience*, VIII, 130–32
—*The Vision of the Last Judgment*, XI, 63, 72

Blindness
and castration, VII, 137, 163n37
in *Heracles*, VI, 249
as inner light, VIII, 38

in *Lycidas*, II, 124–25
Milton's, VII, 155, 217, 218
and Milton's use of color, III, 73–74
and the moon, IX, 164
in *PL*, II, 214–15; V, 32; X, 107
as St. Paul's affliction, X, 146–48
in *SA*, I, 117, 118–19, 124–25,
    127; II, 222; V, 81; VI, 249;
    X, 15
   in *Second Defence*, VI, 248; VIII,
    91–92, 217, 244; IX, 68–69,
    164–65; X, 147–48
   in *Sonnet 22*, X, 115
   in *Sonnet 23*, IV, 141, 142, 145,
    146; VI, 185, 187, 188; VIII,
    159–60; X, 116
Block books, VII, 273
Bloom, Harold, XI, 45, 70–71, 75,
   76, 77, 124–25
Blount, Charles
   —*The Oracles of Reason*, VII, 242
Blount, Thomas
   —*The Academie of Eloquence*,
    VIII, 255
Blundeville, Thomas, on history, V, 24
Boadicea, IV, 127, 128
Boccaccio
   —*De Genealogiae Deorum*
    gentilium, X, 43
Boccalini, Traiano
   —*Ragguagli di Parnaso*, IV, 118
Bodkin, Maud
   on *PL*, VIII, 20
   on *SA*, III, 62
Boethius, IV, 169
Bompart, Johannes
   —*Parallela Sacra et Profana*, VII,
    245
Book metaphor, in *Areopagitica*, IX,
   190–93, 194
Book of Common Prayer, VI, 302n1
Book of Enoch, VII, 297; VIII,
   186–89

Book of Nature, in *PL*, IV, 32–33;
   V, 183; X, 93, 95. *See also* Nature
Borrow, Dr. Samuel, XI, 9
Boughner, Daniel, on Harapha, IV,
   52; XII, 92
Bower
   in landscape, VIII, 20–21
   in Paradise, V, 54–55, 156–57,
    261–62; VII, 282–83; VIII, 21,
    23–25, 29–30
Bowers, Fredson, on *PL*, V, 236
Bowers, R. H., on *Comus*, VI, 166
Boys, John, VII, 194
Bradshaw, John, VIII, 92; XII,
   176–77
Breasted, Barbara, *III, 201–24*
Bridges, John, VIII, 105
Brief History of Muscovia, IV, 136;
   VII, 247
Brief Notes, VII, 235
Bright, Timothy, I, 153
   —*Treatise of Melancholy*, IV,
    203–04
Brisman, Leslie, *II, 27–35*
Broadbent, J. B., V, 68, 252–53
   on Nativity ode, VII, 174, 175,
    177; IX, 44, 45–46, 67
   on *PL*, V, 230, 231, 250, 262;
    VIII, 95; IX, 56, 66; XII, 7
Brodwin, Leonora Leet, *VI, 21–83;*
   VIII, 165–207
Brooke, Lord, IX, 179
Brooks, Cleanth, XI, 40
   on *L'Allegro*, VII, 81, 83
   on Nativity ode, II, 107
Brotherhood, in *PL*, IV, 6–7, 22
Brothers (*Comus*)
   based on mystery play characters,
    VI, 124–27
   fantasies of, VI, 158–59, 172–74
   intellect of, VI, 15–16
   and Narcissus, VI, 172
   as Puritan ministers, VI, 127–28,
    133–34

Brothers (cont.)
  role played by, V, 291–92,
    297–98, 303
  sincerity of, VI, 153–54
  view of Wood of, VI, 154
Brower, Reuben, on Pope and
    Milton, XI, 29, 36–37
Browne, Sir Thomas, I, 138
Bryskett, Lodowick
  —A Discourse of Civill Life, IX,
    209–10
Buber, Martin, XII, 8
Bullinger, Heinrich, on rule of
    charity, VI, 204–05
Bundy, Murray, on PL, V, 237
Bunyan, John, VII, 229
  —Pilgrim's Progress, II, 218–19;
    IX, 100
Burden, Dennis H., II, 74
  on PL, V, 206; IX, 81, 86, 88, 91,
    92, 94–95, 95–96, 100
Burges, Cornelius, IV, 66
Burke, Kenneth, IV, 110
Burnet, Thomas
  —Archaeologiae Philosophicae,
    VII, 242
Burton, Robert, V, 22; XII, 216
  —Anatomy of Melancholy, I,
    137–38
Busembaum, Hermann
  —Medulla Theologiae Moralis,
    XII, 261
Bush, Douglas, XI, 99–114; I, 48; X,
    36, 37, 39–40
  on Circe, VI, 22
  on PL, III, 159; V, 3
Butler, Samuel, XI, 17
Butts, Thomas, XI, 51
Buxtorf Bible, IV, 196–200
Byron, George Gordon, Lord
  response to Milton of, XI, xi–xiii
  on Satan, XI, 85
  —Cain, XI, xii
  —Manfred, XI, xii

Calepinus, Friar Ambrosius
  —Dictionarium Octo Linguarum,
    X, 41
Calhoun, Thomas O., VI, 165–79
Callimachus
  —Hymns, VII, 169, 174, 175–76,
    180
Calliope, X, 35, 37–38, 60
Callistratus, XII, 201
Calvin, John, IX, 225–26, 227, 228,
    238, 265, 272; X, 94, 95, 106
  on astrology, XII, 225
  on celibacy, VI, 281
  on Moses, VII, 229
  on predestination, XII, 53–55
  on purification of women, VIII,
    155
  on purity of church, VI, 121
  on rebellion, IV, 23
  on rule of charity, VI, 204
  on Satan, IX, 269
  on self-knowledge, III, 106–07
  —Institutes of the Christian
    Religion, XII, 53–55
  —Warning Against So-called
    Judicial Astrology, XII, 225
Calvinism
  doctrine of, XII, 55–56, 57–58
  in PL, XII, 48, 49–50.
  See also Calvin, John
Cambridge manuscript. See Trinity
    manuscript
Cames, Gérard, VII, 278
Campbell, Gordon, IX, 243–60
Campbell, Lily B., V, 6, 24
  on muses, X, 56, 58
Camus, in Lycidas, III, 14, 37
Canon Law
  in Colasterion, VIII, 115–16
  on divorce, VI, 199, 209, 210
Canticum Canticorum. See Song of
    Solomon
Canzone, Milton's treatment of, V,
    129, 138–39

Cardan, Jerome, XII, 213, 225
Carena, Cesare, XII, 215–16
Carey, John
  on Clio, X, 39
  on *Comus*, IX, 49
  on *PL*, V, 260
  on *PR*, XII, 256
Carolus Stephanus
  —*Dictionarium Historicum ac
    Poeticum*, X, 41
Cartwright, Thomas, IV, 81; VI, 124
  —*A Treatise of Christian Religion*,
    IX, 254
Casa, Giovanni della
  —*Rime e Prose*, VII, 143
Cassiodorus, VII, 86
Castlehaven scandal, III, 202, 203–
  05, 211–17
  Milton's knowledge of, III, 217–18
  public response to, III, 218–19
Castle of Perseverance, The, VI, 125
Castration, IX, 47–48, 67–69
  and blindness, VII, 137, 163n37
Catalogue convention
  in hymns, VII, 180–81
  in *Lycidas*, III, 15–16, 63–65
  in Nativity ode, IV, 171, 174
  in *PL*, I, 34–37; IX, 113, 114
  in Virgil, I, 33–34
Catharsis
  defined, II, 215–16
  in *Lycidas*, VIII, 53
  in *PL*, II, 214–16
  as physical purgation, II, 217–22
  as regeneration, II, 216, 219
  in *SA*, II, 219–30
Catholicism, and tyranny, IV, 124
Cats, Jacob, VI, 278–79
  —*Tafereel van de Belacchende
    Werelt*, XII, 203
  —*Trou-ringh*, VI, 278–79.
  See also Barlaeus, Caspar
Catullus
  epithalamia of, V, 40, 41, 42–47,

52, 53, 54, 57
  Hesperus in, VI, 265
  as influence in *PL*, V, 42–47, 52,
    53, 54, 57
Cecil, Sir William, IV, 86
Celibacy
  Calvin on, VI, 281
  in *Epitaphium Damonis*, VII, 131
  Milton's, VII, 144, 150–51.
  See also Chastity
Ceremony
  in Old and New Dispensations,
    VIII, 153–56
  purpose of, XII, 145.
  See also Baptism; Mass; Ritual
Ceres, in *PL*, V, 161–62
Chambers, A. B., *VII, 189–205*
  on *PR*, XII, 197
  on *SA*, IX, 186, 198; X, 23
Chambers, E. K., IV, 96
Chambers, Sir William, VIII, 10, 16
Chanson de Roland, VIII, 74
Chaos, I, 11, 156–57; II, 64–65;
  VIII, 20, 36–37, 172–74; XI, 42–
  43, 46; XII, 11–12, 20
Chapman, George, IV, 130; VIII,
  74, 82
Chappell, William, VII, 135–36
Chariots
  in Nativity ode, IV, 168
  in *PL*, III, 66–67, 76, 173–77, 178;
    IX, 52–58, 66–67; XII, 230
Charity, A. C., on typology, VI, 195
Charity, VI, 51–52
  lack of, in *Comus*, VI, 51–52
  lack of, in *PR*, VI, 52
  St. Paul on, VI, 204
  in *Tetrachordon*, VI, 209, 210,
    211.
  See also Rule of charity
Charles I, IV, 44, 56, 123, 124; V,
  279
Charles II, V, 262, 276
Charles, R. H., VIII, 186

Chastity, V, 123, 124; XII, 34–35
in *An Apology,* V, 118–19, 121;
VI, 42; VIII, 83
in *Comus,* III, 206–10; VI, 50–53,
80–81*n47,* 123–24, 173; VII,
148–49
in *Elegy* 6, VI, 40
in *PL,* IV, 9
patristic teachers on, VI, 123
and virginity, VII, 148–50
Chaucer, Geoffrey
Alcestis in, X, 130–32
—*Legend of Good Women,* X,
130–32
—*Squire's Tale,* IX, 215–16
Cherubim, IX, 53
Chester plays, VI, 134–35; XII, 99
"Child-bed taint," in *Sonnet 23,* IV,
143–45. *See also* Purification
Chivalric tales
in *L'Allegro* and *Il Penseroso,* IX,
212–13
heroism in, II, 157; IX, 106–09
Milton on, VIII, 83–84, 88–89
Choice, in reading *PL,* I, 6, 26–28;
II, 32; IX, 90. *See also* Ambiguity;
Multiple choice
Choice, moral
in *Comus,* IX, 27
and freedom, IV, 108
in *PL,* VI, 11–14, 17, 56
in *PR,* VII, 42–43
in *Sonnet 7,* VIII, 45.
See also Free will
Chorus (*SA*)
antifeminism of, I, 129–30
as audience of tragedy, XII, 122
and Dalila, X, 26–28
despair of, XII, 153–54
education of, II, 170, 171
function of, VII, 55–57, 59, 66–
71; XII, 142, 144, 148–50
irony of, II, 197
limited vision of, I, 116–22, 125–

26, 129, 131–33; XII, 146–48,
150–53, 153–54, 155–56, 158–
59, 160–61
passivity of, IV, 56–57; VII, 60
regressive movement of, X, 16–17
and Samson, contrasted, I, 116–
22, 125–26, 129, 131–33; XII,
141–63
sonnets of, V, 149–51
and Theseus (*Heracles*), VI,
250–52
Chorus, in Sophocles, X, 9, 11
Christ
and Abdiel, III, 180
and Adam, VII, 268–69, 273, 287,
304–05; IX, 261–63, 265–66,
268–69, 271
and Alcestis, VI, 184
in *An Apology,* VII, 60
and Augustus, I, 32
baptism of, II, 85–87; IX, 267
and Chaos, I, 11
and church, IV, 81–85, 91, 92; V,
120; VI, 122, 186; VII, 281–82;
XII, 30–35
and David, XII, 125–26
development of, in *PR,* II, 84–85;
VII, 42–44
in *De Doctrina Christiana,* V,
202–03; VIII, 201; IX, 264–65
early life of, XII, 239–40
and Eve, IV, 185–86; V, 143; VI,
19; IX, 141–42
and Hercules, VI, 184–85; VIII,
156
heroism of, II, 85, 90; VI, 106;
IX, 8
horoscope of, XII, 213–33
humanity of, VI, 229; XII, 235–
37, 240
as image of God, VIII, 242
irony of, V, 90
knowledge of, IX, 265–68
light of, IX, 159–61

in literature, II, 3
in *Lycidas,* III, 44; IV, 155; V, 77;
  IX, 43, 223–24
meditations of, II, 91–94
messianic function of, II, 7
militarism of, XII, 246–47
and the moon, IX, 158–64
and Moses, II, 12–14; V, 69, 75;
  VII, 209, 224–27; IX, 226
as narrator of *PR,* II, 88–89
in Nativity ode, IV, 165–66, 168,
  171, 173, 174; V, 77
and Pan, IV, 169–70
in *PR,* I, 62–64; II, 84–85, 92–93;
  IV, 178–92; V, 70, 203; VII,
  197, 200–01; XII, 21–22
and purification, II, 226
republicanism of, XII, 245–46
rhetoric of, I, 90
and Samson, II, 224, 227–28; III,
  194, 196; V, 79; XII, 104–05
Socinian view of, VIII, 201
soliloquies of, VI, 233–35; VII,
  197, 200–01; IX, 266
sonnets of, V, 147–48
temptations of, I, 62; II, 88, 95–
  99; IV, 178–93; VI, 65–68,
  218–21, 228; VII, 43–44, 94–
  96, 202; IX, 264–65, 268–70
as *Theanthropos,* VII, 199–200,
  202.
  See also *Paradise Regained;* Son;
  Typology
Christian Doctrine. See *De Doctrina
Christiana*
Christianity, ambivalence of, II, 104,
  106–07, 109
Christopher, G. B., on *Lycidas,* IX,
  228
Christ's College, Cambridge
  Milton at, VII, 135–38
  Pammachius presented at, VI, 118
Chronos, defined, VII, 189, 190–92;
  XII, 197. See also Time

Church
  in *Areopagitica,* I, 150
  Calvin on, VI, 121
  and Christ, IV, 81–85, 91, 92; V,
    120; VI, 122, 186; VII, 281–82;
    XII, 30–35
  in *Comus,* VI, 127–28
  in *De Doctrina Christiana,* IV, 81–
    85; VI, 122; VII, 281, 282
  and Eve, XII, 29–35
  in iconography, VII, 281–82
  inviolability of, VI, 127–28
  and moon, IX, 155–56
  in *The Reason of Church-
    Government,* IV, 82–83, 92–93
  universal, VI, 120–24
  visible and invisible, IV, 81–85;
    VI, 121–22; VII, 282–83.
  See also Lady Wandering in the
    Wilderness
Cicero
  —*Brutus,* II, 135
  —*Orator,* II, 134, 135–36
  —*De Oratore,* I, 74; II, 134–35;
    VIII, 72, 73–74; X, 180, 181
  —*Somnium Scipionis,* XII, 39–40
Circe, VI, 21–83, 119
  in *L'Allegro* and *Il Penseroso,* VI,
    43–46
  in *An Apology,* VI, 41–43, 54
  in Ariosto, VI, 26–28
  in *Comus,* V, 304; VI, 46–54, 130–
    31, 170; IX, 64
  in *Eikonoklastes,* VI, 54
  in *Elegy 1,* VI, 38–39; VII, 139
  in *Elegy 6,* VI, 39–40
  in *Elegy 7,* VI, 39, 59
  in Gelli, VI, 35–36, 55
  in Homer, VI, 22–26
  and liberty, VI, 54–58
  in *Lycidas,* VI, 39
  Ovid on, VI, 24–25, 25–26, 36–37
  in *PL,* VI, 54–65
  in *PR,* VI, 65–68

Circe *(cont.)*
  as political symbol, VI, 54–58,
    66–68
  in *Prolusion 7*, VI, 40–41
  in Renaissance mythography, VI,
    22–23
  and Roman church, VI, 130–31
  in *SA*, VI, 68–75
  Sandys on, VI, 36–37
  and Satan, VI, 55–57
  in *Sonnet 12*, VI, 55
  in Spenser, VI, 31–36, 78nn23, 24
  in Tasso, VI, 28–31
  temptations of, defined, VI, 23–26
Circuitus spiritualis, V, 181, 184, 186
Upon the Circumcision, V, 104
Cirillo, Albert R., *III, 83–102*
  on noon, VI, 268
  on *PL*, IX, 158
Clark, Donald Lemen
  on Milton's education, X, 178
  on rhetoric, I, 68
Clark, E. M., on *PL*, V, 254
Clement of Alexandria, VII, 216;
    XII, 260
Climax, in *PL*, III, 144–45
Clio, X, 35–37, 39–48, 51, 58–59, 60
Cloppenburg
  —*Compendiolum Socinianismi
    Confutatum*, VIII, 194–95
Clouds, in Blake's *Milton*, XI, 62–63
Cohen, Kitty, *III, 159–84*
Cohen, Ralph, VIII, 123
Colaccio, John J., *VI, 181–97*
  on *Sonnet 23*, X, 112–13
Colasterion, VI, 203
  Canon Law in, VIII, 115–16
  heroism in, VIII, 85
  imagery of, VIII, 116–17
  irony in, VIII, 115
  Marprelate influence in, VIII,
    114–19
  occasion of, VIII, 114
  puns in, VIII, 117

  satires in, VIII, 85
Coleridge, Samuel Taylor
  on decorum, I, 3
  on history play, V, 25
  on imagination, V, 72–73
  on Milton, XI, 69, 83, 85–86;
    XII, 47
  and Wordsworth, XI, 86–87
  —*Biographia Literaria*, V, 72–73
  —"Letters on the Spaniards," XI,
    85
  —*The Statesman's Manual*, XI,
    85–86
Colet, John
  on Creation, I, 156
  on reading Scripture, X, 56
  —*Letters to Radulphus on the
    Mosaic Creation*, I, 156
Colie, Rosalie, XII, 79, 117
Colish, Marcia, X, 103
Collins, Dan S., *V, 229–48*
Collins, William
  —"Ode on the Poetical Charac-
    ter," VI, 259
  —"Ode to Evening," VI, 259
Color
  in Homer, III, 56, 57, 68, 69
  iconography of, III, 55–60, 61–67
  Milton's use of, III, 55–81, 154–55
  perception of, III, 67
  in Virgil, III, 56, 57, 62, 65, 68–69
Colossians, III, 179
Comedy
  in *Colasterion*, VIII, 114–19
  in Greek drama, X, 7–14
  in Homer, X, 5–6
  in *PL*, I, 22–23, 24–26, 104, 106,
    113; V, 18, 24, 27, 44–45; VIII,
    215, 230–35; X, 5, 68, 69–70
  in *SA*, I, 122, 123, 130; X, 14–16,
    27; XII, 92.
  See also Parody; Puns; Satire
Comes, Natalis
  —*Mythologiae*, X, 37, 38

Committee for Trade, XII, 171

Committee for Trade and Foreign
Affairs, XII, 169–80

Commonplace Book, I, 21; II, 141;
IV, 46, 120–21, 123; XII, 220, 261

Communication
importance of, IX, 4, 6–7
in *SA*, X, 30–31, 32

Communion
and food, I, 140–43, 144
Milton on, I, 140–41

Comus, V, 88; IX, 106
adolescence in, VI, 169–72, 174–77
allegory in, V, 120
Antichrist in, VI, 129, 132
and antiprelatical tracts, V, 94–97, 104, 109, 110, 111, 118
audience of, III, 202, 205
Bacchus legend in, VI, 131–32
and Castlehaven scandal, III, 201–24
chastity in, III, 206–10; VI, 50–53, 80–81n47, 123–24, 173; VII, 148–49
church in, VI, 127–28
Circe in, V, 304; VI, 46–54, 130–31, 170; IX, 64
color in, III, 57, 58, 61, 62, 66, 69, 76
contraries in, VII, 32–36
control in, VI, 154–55
Cupid in, VI, 134
dance in, VI, 146–47; VII, 34, 151–52
dragon in, IX, 48
as drama of three age groups, VI, 165–79
Echo in, V, 296; VI, 159–60, 171–72
education in, V, 298–99
ending of, VII, 151–52
epilogue of, V, 306; VI, 134, 161–63; VII, 150, 158

and *Epitaphium Damonis*, VII, 128
faith in, VI, 122–23
family in, VI, 168–69, 170, 177
first production of, III, 201–02, 205, 219; V, 291; VI, 167–69
free will in, VI, 15–16
Gorgon in, VII, 243; IX, 49, 63–64
haemony and moly in, IV, 156–57; V, 96, 298–99; VI, 174, 177; IX, 65–66
hell in, VI, 148
Hermes in, VI, 133
Hesperides in, IX, 48
imagery of, V, 122
inversion in, VII, 35–36
knowledge in, V, 290
lack of charity in, VI, 51–52
and Lady Wandering in the Wilderness, VI, 120–21, 122–23, 124, 127–28
landscape in, II, 38; VI, 143–64; VII, 33; VIII, 13–14
Lawes portrayed in, V, 290, 291, 292, 296, 299, 303, 305–06
light in, VI, 155–56; VII, 34
magic in, VI, 174
manuscripts of, III, 205–11; VI, 129, 167; VII, 147–50
moral choice in, IX, 27
motto of, VII, 153–54; VIII, 58
music in, V, 294, 307; IX, 65–66
and mystery plays, VI, 114–42
Narcissus in, VI, 172
nature in, VI, 16–17, 143–46; VII, 33
Neoplatonism in, VI, 129
Neptune in, V, 292; VI, 147
organicism in, IV, 83
and Orpheus, IX, 43–44
parody in, VII, 32–36
pastoral in, V, 120
Philomela in, VI, 171–72

Comus (cont.)
  Platonism in, V, 120
  plot of, III, 203
  and Pope's *Dunciad*, XI, 44
  publication of, III, 203; VIII,
    57–58, 61
  puns in, IX, 46
  realism in, VI, 148
  and *The Reason of Church-
    Government*, V, 94, 97, 109
  and *Of Reformation*, V, 95-97,
    104, 109
  regeneracy in, V, 97, 107, 112,
    120, 124
  and Revelation, VI, 115
  rhetoric in, VI, 16–17
  St. Michael in, VI, 133
  Scylla and Charybdis in, VI, 108
  sensuality in, IX, 26
  1738 stage adaptation of, XI, 69
  sexuality in, VI, 175–77; VII,
    148–49
  shepherds in, VI, 154–55
  skill and virtue in, V, 123, 289–
    308
  sonnets in, V, 152*n*2
  student responses to, VI, 166
  sun in, IX, 46, 63–66; XII, 230
  symbolic process in, V, 74
  syncretism in, VI, 129–30, 134,
    136
  tableaux in, VI, 157–58
  Thyrsis in, IV, 156
  as tragicomedy, V, 20
  Virgil's influence in, VII, 153-54
  virtue in, V, 123
  water in, VIII, 18.
  See also Attendant Spirit;
    Brothers; Comus; Lady; Sabrina
Comus
  as adolescent, VI, 169–70, 175
  deceit of, VI, 150–51
  destructiveness of, VII, 33–34
  diction of, VI, 151–52

  skill of, V, 290, 293–94, 296–97,
    300–01, 302
Conklin, George Newton, and *De
  Doctrina Christiana*, VIII, 197
Consciousness, and evil, XII, 10–22
*Considerations Touching the Likeli-
  est Means*, IV, 93; VIII, 55, 158;
  X, 182, 185
Contemplation, III, 103–04, 107;
  IX, 125
  and landscape, VIII, 28–29
  in *Lycidas*, III, 42
  in *PL*, I, 36
  in *PR*, VIII, 29
  in *Il Penseroso*, VIII, 28
  in Tasso, III, 84–85, 86, 89–91,
    92–94, 96, 98, 100.
  See also Action and contempla-
    tion; Self-knowledge
Conti, Natale, on Circe, VI, 22, 36, 55
Contraries
  in Blake, VIII, 128
  Milton's use of, I, 90–91; VII,
    36–42, 44–45
Control, in *Comus*, VI, 154–55
Controversy, Milton's dislike of, X,
  182–83
Conversation. *See* Communication;
  Language; Speech
Cook, Albert S., IV, 168; VII, 172
  on Nativity ode, VII, 167
  on *PL*, VIII, 253, 264
Cook, Captain James, VII, 246
Cooper, Bishop Thomas, VIII, 105
  on Calliope, X, 37
Cope, Jackson I., *I, 51–65*
  on language, II, 178–79
  on *PL*, IX, 78–88; X, 96; XII, 76
Copernican Revolution, Milton on,
  VI, 85–86, 95–96, 101–02; XII,
  230–31
Corinthians, Epistles to. *See* Paul, St.
Cornford, Francis Macdonald, XII, 95
Corpus mysticum, IV, 81–85

Corruption
in antiprelatical tracts, V, 87–127
in *Lycidas,* V, 88
Cotton, John, XII, 32, 34
Council, Norman B., *IX, 203–19*
Council in Heaven, III, 161–71; V,
28; VIII, 276–79
Council of State, V, 272; XII, 165–89
Covenant theology, VII, 236–37
Cowley, Abraham, XII, 262
Cowper, William, XI, 69
Cox, Lee Sheridan, on *SA,* IX, 48–49
Coytmor, Robert, XII, 173–74, 179
Creation
of Adam, V, 239–40; VII, 270–77
Colet on, I, 156
and Crucifixion, VII, 279–81
Dionysius on, I, 155–56
in *De Doctrina Christiana,* I, 149–
51, 153, 154; V, 196; VIII,
173–74
of Eve, V, 240–41; VII, 270–71;
X, 117
and Fall of Man, XII, 4–5
in Genesis, VIII, 224
in the Hermetica, I, 158
Hesiod on, I, 151–52
light and dark in, III, 61
Lucretius on, I, 152
as mystery, VI, 105
organicism of, I, 150–64
Plato on, I, 153-54
in rabbinical tradition, IV, 200–08
as reflection of God, IV, 32–36
St. Basil on, I, 152–53
sense metaphors in, II, 180–81
Spirit in, I, 149–57; III, 30–31
Creativity, IV, 7, 11; IX, 15–16;
XII, 3–4
Creator, identity of, in *PL,* VI, 103
Criticism, IV, 3–4; V, 67
bibliographical, VII, 26n2
biographical, II, 105; IV, 141–42;
VI, 181–82, 186; VIII, 149–50

close reading in, VII, 30
Crocean, VII, 11, 26n2
current trends in, VII, viii–ix
defensiveness in, IX, 7
experiential, VII, 95–98
feminist, VI, 3–5; VIII, 219n7;
IX, 12, 28
formalist, VII, 95–96
generic, VII, 30
hindsight in, VIII, 51–52
historical, IV, 40–41; VII, ix, 10–
11, 18–22, 23–24, 165–66
in illustrations, VIII, 123–24
intuition in, VII, 6–8, 9–10
issues of, IX, 3–4
mythic, II, 3, 6; VII, 29–30; IX,
78–88
necessity of, VII, 19–20
of *PL,* I, 1–3, 15–16, 22; IX, 77–
103
of *PR,* I, 52, 61
post-Romantic, II, 60
rhetorical, IX, 89–101
of *SA,* VII, 49–50; XII, 118–19
in sixteenth and seventeenth
centuries, VII, 17
sociological, VI, 4–5
of *Sonnet 19,* X, 141, 142
structural, VII, 29–30
subjective, IX, 89–90
textural, VII, ix.
See also Methodologies
Croll, Morris, IV, 131–32; V, 274
Cromwell, Oliver, IV, 40–41, 43, 50–
52, 54–56, 57–58; V, 271; VIII,
92–93; X, 171; XII, 170, 181–84,
186
Cromwell, Richard, V, 271
Crown, VII, 294–95
Crucifixion, VI, 185, 223; IX, 269,
271; XI, 74
in *Biblia Pauperum,* VII, 273
and Creation, VII, 279–81
in iconography, VII, 305

Cudworth, Ralph
—A Treatise Concerning Eternal
  and Immutable Morality, III, 113
Cullmann, Oscar, VII, 190
"Cultum institutum," VII, 245, 248,
  253, 255, 262
Culture, IX, 15, 41
Cupid
  in Areopagitica, VII, 36–37
  in Bartas, V, 57
  in Comus, VI, 134
  in epithalamic tradition, V, 47
  in PL, V, 56–57
Cursor Mundi, X, 30
Curtius, Ernst Robert
  on "bucolic repose," II, 45–46
  on gardens, V, 253
  on the Iliad, VIII, 74
  on muses, X, 35, 36, 56, 57–58
  on Nativity ode, VII, 171, 172

Daemons, VI, 132–33
Dagon, IX, 47
  and Dalila, XII, 98
  and Sin, VII, 44
Daiches, David
  on Elegy 1, VI, 38–39
  on Lycidas, IV, 52
  on PL, III, 159, 166
Dalila, I, 120, 126–29
  as adequate antagonist, XII, 97
  and Chorus, X, 26–28
  as Circe, VI, 69–70, 72–73
  conversion of, III, 188, 189–90
  and Dagon, XII, 98
  as deviant, IX, 29–30
  and Helen, I, 128–29
  and Hera, VI, 252
  language of, II, 185, 186–88
  and Mosaic law, XII, 154–55
  motives of, X, 23–33
  name of, XII, 97
  and Samson, I, 126–28; X, 24–26,
    28; XII, 98–99, 100

and Satan, XII, 99
and Sin, XII, 98
as stereotype, IX, 30–33
sympathetic views of, X, 28–30
as temptress, II, 161–64; IV, 42
Damico, Helen, XII, 91–116
Damon, S. Foster, XI, 72; XII, 19
Dance, in Comus, VI, 146–47; VII,
  34, 151–52
Daniel, Book of, VI, 237; X, 81, 83,
  85; XI, 63, 73
Daniel, Samuel, IV, 133, 134–35
Daniells, Roy
  on Lycidas, IX, 224, 239
  on PL, V, 200
  on PR, XII, 93
  on SA, XII, 93
Daniélou, Jean, on Moses, VII, 225
Danielson, Dennis, XII, 47–73
Dante
  on delight, VI, 190–91
  on evil, VI, 5
  on glory, X, 52–53
  on intellect, VI, 188, 189
  paradise of, II, 38–39, 49
  wood of, VI, 146
  —Divina Commedia, XI, 76–77
  —Inferno, III, 60; X, 52–53
  —Purgatorio, I, 37; VI, 193; X, 53
Darkness. See Blindness; Light;
  Shade
D'Avenant, Sir William
  —Gondibert, IX, 107
Davenport, John, IV, 54
David, and Christ, XII, 125–26
Davie, Donald, on PL, I, 7
Davies, Sir John
  —"Orchestra," XII, 203–04
Davila, Enrico
  —History of the Civil Wars of
    France, IV, 123
Davis, Michael, IV, 102
Dawn, in L'Allegro, VII, 79–80, 81
Dead Sea apples, VII, 252–53

Death, allegorical figure of (*PL*)
  and Adam and Eve, VII, 289, 298
  birth of, VI, 110; VII, 296–97
  and Fall of Man, II, 53
  in infernal trinity, V, 145–46; VII, 39; IX, 23–24
  jaws of, VIII, 175–76
  kinship relations of, IV, 10–11
  mortality of, VIII, 177–78
  in *PL*, VII, 242–43, 250, 253
  as predator, VII, 287–88
  and Satan, I, 41–42, 84–85
  and Sin, I, 11, 84–85; V, 80; VIII, 176, 178, 179–80
Death
  Adam and Eve's discussion of, V, 223
  Belial on, VIII, 178, 182
  in *Lycidas*, IV, 157–58
  and Paradise, V, 197
  in *PL*, II, 33; VII, 242
  Satan's statement of, V, 218
  spiritual, II, 152
On the Death of a Fair Infant
  and *An Apology*, V, 110
  color in, III, 58
  pastoral in, V, 119
  regeneracy in, V, 103
Debate, in Milton, VI, 295
De Brass, Henry, Milton's exchange with, IV, 119–20
Deception, in *PL*, I, 8. *See also* Truth
Decorum, I, 3
De Doctrina Christiana. See under *Doctrina*
Defence of the People of England. See *Defences*
Defences, I, 20–21; X, 182
  civic fortitude in, VIII, 90, 91–92
  imagery of, IV, 59–60
  —*First Defence*, XII, 236–37
    Hercules in, XII, 244
    heroism in, VIII, 89–90

  military imagery in, IV, 59
  Samson in, IV, 40
  Tacitus' influence in, IV, 119, 120, 125–27
  —*Second Defence*, VI, 203, 248; VIII, 54
  and antiprelatical tracts, V, 90
  astrology in, XII, 214
  authority in, X, 186
  blindness in, VI, 248; VII, 91–92, 217, 244; IX, 68–69, 164–65; X, 147–48
  Cromwell in, IV, 55; VIII, 92–93
  gardening in, V, 252
  heroism in, VIII, 90–94
  Homer in, VIII, 91–92
  liberty in, V, 269–70
  military imagery of, IV, 59–60
  Milton's vocational choice in, VIII, 65–66
  New Model Army in, IV, 52
  puns in, VIII, 91
  St. Paul in, X, 145
  self-esteem in, VIII, 243–44
  Tacitus' influence in, IV, 126
Definition, Milton's rhetorical use of, X, 193n23
Defoe, Daniel
  on *PL*, VI, 277–78
  —*Review of the State of the British Nation*, VI, 277–78
Deformity, in myth, IX, 69. *See also* Blindness
Deity. *See* God
"Delight"
  Aquinas on, VI, 190
  in Dante, VI, 190–91
  in *Sonnet 23*, VI, 190–92
Della Casa, Giovanni
  —*Rime e Prose*, VII, 143
Dendy, Edward, XII, 173, 184, 187
Denham, Sir John
  —*Cooper's Hill*, II, 43; X, 201

Derketo, XII, 98

Despair, I, 71–72
  and hope, I, 80, 82–83, 85, 86
  in *SA*, XII, 153–54, 156, 159, 161

Dessau Psalter, VII, 279

Deuteronomy, IX, 226
  divorce in, VI, 208, 209
  Moses in, VII, 225
  as source for *PL*, III, 178

Deviance, social, IX, 10–11, 19–21

Dianoia
  in epic theory, I, 70–71
  in Milton's epics, I, 88–89
  in Plato, VI, 217

Di Cesare, Mario A., *I, 31–50*

Didache, VIII, 204n23

Diekhoff, John
  on *Comus*, III, 206; VI, 169
  on *PL*, V, 205–06

Digression, in *PL*, VI, 285–86

Diodati, Charles
  death of, VII, 158
  indulgence of, VII, 139–40
  later education of, VII, 141–42
  letters to Milton of, VII, 134–35
  as subject of *Epitaphium
    Damonis*, VII, 127–33
  youth of, VII, 133–34

Diodati, John, VII, 133, 158, 193

Diodorus Siculus, II, 138–39; V,
  256; X, 81–82

Diogenes Laertius, on Plato's dialogues, VI, 216

Dionysius of Halicarnassus, II, 136

Dionysius the Areopagite, I, 154,
  155–56

Dionysus, X, 13–14; XII, 14

Di Salvo, Jackie, *IV, 39–62*
  on *SA*, XII, 136

Discipline, IV, 53–54

Disease, metaphors of, II, 217–22,
  225; V, 91, 109–10, 116–17

Disguise
  in parody, VII, 35

Satan's, I, 76, 79, 95–96, 110,
  111-12

Dissonance, in Nativity ode, IV,
  170–71. *See also* Noise

Divorce
  in Canon Law, VI, 199, 209, 210
  and reformation, X, 205–09
  in Scripture, VI, 199–200, 208–
    09, 210.
  See also Divorce tracts; Marriage

Divorce tracts
  rule of charity in, VI, 199–214
  tradition in, I, 19–20.
  See also *Colasterion; Doctrine and
    Discipline of Divorce;
    Judgement of Martin Bucer;
    Tetrachordon*

Docetist heresy, XII, 259

De Doctrina Christiana
  accommodation in, VI, 86, 91–93
  "adhere" in, VII, 275–76
  Antichrist in, VI, 130
  Arminianism in, XII, 63
  astrology in, XII, 216–17
  baptism in, XII, 255
  Bible in, XII, 48
  biblical sources of, VII, 223–24;
    VIII, 191; IX, 244
  Christ in, V, 202–03; VIII, 201;
    IX, 264–65
  church in, IV, 81–85; VI, 122;
    VII, 281, 282
  Communion in, I, 141
  composition of, IX, 253, 255–57
  Creation in, I, 149–51, 153, 154;
    V, 196; VIII, 173–74
  eternal torment in, VIII, 165–66,
    190–202
  evil in, III, 125; VIII, 284–85
  faith in, V, 203–04; VII, 238; IX,
    245–46; X, 169, 170; XII, 69
  Fall of Man in, XII, 61
  "fortitude" in, VII, 292
  free will in, XII, 59–60

gardening imagery in, VII, 280–81

God in, III, 160, 167–68; IV, 28; VII, 240

grace in, XII, 59–60, 61, 63

hell in, VIII, 171–72, 174

history in, V, 203

"image" in, VIII, 225–27

incompleteness of, IX, 250–53, 257

ingrafting in Christ in, IV, 154–55; VII, 280

Last Judgment in, VIII, 169, 190–92

law in, VII, 235–37, 261; XII, 143–44

manuscript of, IX, 250, 255

marriage in, V, 55; VII, 277

mortalist heresy in, VIII, 167, 173–74

Moses in, VII, 210–11, 215–16, 225–26; IX, 234–35

Old and New Dispensations in, IV, 143–44; VII, 223–24

organicism in, VI, 122

original sin in, VII, 244–45

"paradise within" in, V, 201–05

"Perfect Glorification" in, V, 201–05

prayer in, VII, 227; X, 169

purification in, VIII, 154–55

purpose of, IX, 243–44

rabbinical sources of, IV, 200–02

redemption in, VII, 306

regeneracy in, II, 152, 157, 160, 227–28; V, 203–04; VII, 54

resurrection in, VIII, 195–96

and Revelation, VIII, 190–92

sacraments in, VII, 256

salvation in, II, 226

sin in, VII, 296

Spirit in, I, 148; III, 29; VII, 228–29

structure of, IX, 243–60

temperance in, II, 221

temptation in, II, 157

transitions in, IX, 250, 252, 254

Tree of Knowledge in, VII, 235–37, 254, 255

Tree of Life in, VII, 248

Trinity in, XII, 254

truth in, VI, 86, 91–93

wisdom in, X, 170

Doctrine and Discipline of Divorce

analogy in, X, 205–07, 208

Arminianism in, XII, 60

and Ascham's "Of Marriage," X, 195–215

authority in, X, 184

heroism in, VIII, 84

law in, VII, 235

marriage in, VI, 10–11

Moses in, VII, 219, 226; VIII, 84; IX, 234

"overdated" in, XII, 204–05

rabbinical sources of, IV, 197–200

response to, X, 202, 209

rhetoric of, X, 192, 201–02

rule of charity in, VI, 200, 204, 205–06, 208, 209, 210–11

rule of justice in, X, 207–08

second edition of, VI, 211; X, 204–05

Donne, John, V, 51; VII, 44; VIII, 224; XI, 126; XII, 34, 40

celestial music in, IV, 169, 170

on Crucifixion, VII, 279, 280

medical imagery of, 217–18, 219, 224–25

on Psalms, XII, 125

on Puritans, IV, 89, 90, 91

on Tree of Knowledge, VII, 268

—*The Anniversaries*, XI, 14, 16

—*Devotions Upon Emergent Occasions*, II, 217–18, 219, 224–25

—*Elegy IV*, VI, 165–66

—*Sermons*, IV, 90, 91

Dorian, D. C., on *Sonnet 19*, X, 151

Dorset, First Earl of (Thomas
    Sackville), XI, 8
Dove, John, XII, 32
Dove
    —in Nativity ode, IV, 165–68
    —in PR, IV, 182
Dowey, Edward, X, 94
Downame, John, IV, 47
Dracontius, paradise of, II, 39
Dragon
    and Antichrist, VI, 128
    in Comus, IX, 48
    in mythology, IX, 48–49
    in Nativity ode, IV, 171
    in SA, IX, 48
Drama
    genres of, V, 4
    heroic, I, 55–56, 58–60, 62
    Milton and, V, 4–5
    and ritual, I, 52, 62
Drayton, Michael
    —Endimion and Phoebe, IX, 153
    —"Moses His Birth and Miracles,"
        IX, 230
Dread, XII, 9–10
Dreams
    Adam's, X, 82–83
    Eve's, V, 233, 234–36, 237; XII,
        25–45
    Nebuchadnezzar's, X, 80–81, 83–88
Druce, George C.
    —The Flora of Buckinghamshire,
        V, 259–60
Drugs, in Circean temptation, VI,
    23–24, 31. See also Haemony;
    Moly
Dryden, John, I, 186, 187
    career of, XI, 3, 10, 19–22
    conservatism of, XI, 23
    epigrams for PL of, XI, 4–5
    on free will, XI, 10
    and Sir Robert Howard, XI, 6
    knowledge of Milton's juvenilia
        of, XI, 5

    on language of poetry, XI, 17, 18
    on literary history, XI, 19
    and Milton, I, 54, 60–61; XI,
        vii–viii, 3–27
    Milton's knowledge of, XI, 6–10
    music in, XI, 16
    on PL, XI, 8, 17–19, 24
    projected epic of, XI, 20–22
    on rhyme, I, 53–54
    —Absalom and Achitophel, XI,
        12–13
    —All for Love, I, 54
    —The Conquest of Granada, I, 54,
        55–57, 58–60, 62
    —"Discourse," XI, 17–19, 20–21
    —Eleanora, XI, 14
    —An Essay of Dramatic Poesy, I,
        53; XI, 6
    —Fables, XI, 19, 21–22, 25
    —The Hind and the Panther, XI,
        13–14
    —The Indian Emperour, I, 53, 55
    —King Arthur, XI, 20
    —Mac Flecknoe, XI, 7, 10–12
    —"To the Memory of Mr. Old-
        ham," XI, 15
    —"Ode on the Death of Mr.
        Henry Purcell," XI, 14–16
    —preface to Aureng-Zebe, I, 54;
        XI, 7
    —The Rival Ladies, I, 53; XI, 7
    —The State of Innocence, I, 54;
        V, 5; XI, 8–9, 10, 14, 17
    —Virgil, XI, 20
Dualism, I, 153–54
Du Bartas, Guillaume de Salluste.
    See Bartas, Guillaume de Salluste
    du
Duncan, Joseph
    on location of Eden, X, 77
    on PL, VII, 248
Dunster, Charles
    —Considerations on Milton's
        Early Reading, X, 35

Dürer, Albrecht, VI, 128
Durkheim, Emile, VII, 247, 248
Durkin, Sister Mary Brian, *III,*
  139-58
Dutch Manifesto of July 1652, XII,
  167

Eagle, XI, 77
Ebionism, XII, 16, 18-19, 259
Ecclesiasticus, Moses in, VII, 214
Echo, in *Comus,* V, 296; VI, 159-60,
  171-72
Eden. *See* Paradise
Education
  of Adam, I, 45, 148; II, 53, 54;
    V, 140-42, 241-43; VI, 301;
    X, 95-100, 102-03
  in *L'Allegro* and *Il Penseroso,* IX,
    209-18
  in *An Apology,* V, 117-18
  in *Areopagitica,* VI, 220, 221
  Comenian reforms in, IX, 204,
    206
  in *Comus,* V, 298-99
  of Eve, IV, 13-14; V, 243-45;
    X, 98
  and liberty, IV, 106
  in *Lycidas,* III, 3-34
  Milton on, V, 210; IX, 203-19
  in *PL,* III, 140-41, 155-56; VI,
    7; IX, 208
  in *Ad Patrem,* IX, 207
  in *Prolusion 3,* IX, 205-06
  in *Prolusion 7,* IX, 204, 206-07
  in *Readie and Easie Way,* V, 283
  in *SA,* II, 149-74, 207-09; XII,
    118-19, 146-60.
  See also *Of Education*
Of Education, III, 6; IX, 205, 207;
  XII, 261
  Aristotle in, V, 8
  heroism in, VIII, 81-82
  history in, II, 131
  and Isocrates, IV, 106-08

poetry in, I, 176-77
reading lists in, I, 18
rhetoric in, X, 177-78, 179-80
wisdom and strength in, VII, 51
Egan, James, *VIII, 103-21*
Egerton, Alice, Countess Dowager
  of Derby, III, 214-16, 218,
  220n2
Egerton, John, Earl of Bridgewater,
  III, 214; V, 291, 292-93, 305-06;
  VI, 168
Egerton, John, Viscount Brackley,
  VI, 168, 178
Egerton, Lady Alice, III, 202, 203,
  205, 206, 207; VI, 48, 168, 169,
  178
Egerton, Thomas, VI, 168, 178
Ego integrity, II, 180
Eikon Basilike, VIII, 88
Eikonoklastes, X, 182
  antitraditionalism in, I, 21
  Circe in, VI, 54
  contemporary reputation of, V,
    270-71
  heroism in, VIII, 88-89
  "overdated" in, XII, 205
Eisenstein, Sergei, on *PL,* II, 42
Elegy 1
  and *L'Allegro* and *Il Penseroso,*
    VI, 43
  autobiographical content of, VII,
    133, 134, 135-36, 138-39
  Circe in, VI, 38-39; VII, 139
  darkness in, III, 73
  elegiac poets in, V, 119
  Ovid's influence on, VI, 38-39
  puns in, VII, 137-38
  and *The Reason of Church-
    Government,* V, 115
Elegy 3
  color in, III, 62
  elegiac poets in, V, 119
  regeneracy in, V, 102, 103, 104,
    107, 124

Elegy 4
  and *An Apology*, V, 110
  Clio in, X, 36, 37, 39, 42–43
  minister in, VIII, 210
  and *The Reason of Church-*
    Government, V, 109
  and *Of Reformation*, V, 108
  regeneracy in, V, 107, 124
Elegy 5, III, 75; V, 41, 119; IX,
  45–46
Elegy 6
  and *An Apology*, V, 110
  biographical content of, VII, 134,
    139–40, 146
  chastity in, VI, 40
  Circe in, VI, 39–40
  color in, III, 68
  epic in, VIII, 72
  Milton's poetic vocation in, VIII,
    43
  Nativity ode in, VII, 173
  poet and priest in, IV, 171
  and *The Reason of Church-*
    Government, V, 115
Elegy 7
  autobiographical elements in, VII,
    133, 142–43
  Circe in, VI, 39, 59
  darkness in, III, 73
  dating of, VI, 80*n38*
Eliade, Mircea, I, 184; V, 177; XII,
  4
Eliot, Sir John, IV, 124
Eliot, T. S., XI, viii
  and Milton, XI, xiii–xiv, 115–29
  on *PL*, II, 38
  —*Burnt Norton*, IV, 166
  —*The Cocktail Party*, X, 12; XI,
    127–28
  —*To Criticize the Critic*, XI, 116
  —*The Dry Salvages*, XI, 125, 126
  —*East Coker*, XI, 116–20, 123
  —*The Family Reunion*, XI, 126–
    27

  —*Four Quartets*, IV, 166; XI,
    116–23, 125, 126
  —*Little Gidding*, XI, 120–23
  —*Milton One* ("A Note on the
    Verse of John Milton," 1936),
    XI, 115–16
  —*Milton Two* ("Milton," 1947),
    XI, 115–16
  —*The Waste Land*, XI, 116
Elliott, Emory, *VI, 227–41*
Ellis-Fermor, Una, on *SA*, I, 115;
  II, 225
Ellmann, Richard, XI, viii
Ellwood, Thomas, on *PL*, I, 186–87
Eloquence, Milton on, VIII, 250–52
Elyot, Sir Thomas, I, 138; IX, 204,
  208
Emasculation, in Circean tempta-
  tion, VI, 24–25, 26–27, 29–30, 32,
  62, 65, 70. *See also* Castration
Emblem books, VIII, 29–30; XII,
  203
"Embrace," in *Sonnet 23*, VI, 192–
  93; X, 112–13, 122
Emerson, Ralph Waldo
  on *L'Allegro* and *Il Penseroso*, VI,
    43
  on Fall of Man, XII, 5
Empson, William, IV, 113
  on *PL*, II, 72–73; III, 159; IV, 20;
    V, 257; VI, 301; VIII, 267,
    279; XII, 37, 38, 48
  on *SA*, IX, 29, 31–32; X, 28–29
Enargia, in *Sonnet 18*, X, 173–74
Encomium tôn gamountôn, V, 50–53
Engagement Controversy, X, 211–12
Enoch, Book of, VII, 297; VIII, 184
Entzminger, Robert L., *X, 93–109*
Epanalepsis, in *PL*, III, 147
Ephesians, Epistle to. *See* Paul, St.
Epic, Renaissance theories of, I,
  70–71, 73
Epic awe, I, 45–46, 47
Epic style, I, 3–4

Epic tradition, I, 31–50; VII, 18;
  IX, 105–06; X, 44
  Milton's rejection of, X, 53, 58–61
  in *PL*, II, 212; V, 50–59.
  See also Ariosto; Homer; Spenser;
    Tasso; Virgil
Epigrams, Milton's Latin, IV, 63,
  66, 72–73
Epitaphium Damonis, III, 41; V, 88
  and *An Apology*, V, 110, 111, 119
  astrology in, XII, 214
  autobiographical elements in, VII,
    127–33, 140, 151, 152, 154;
    VIII, 64
  celibacy in, VII, 131
  and *Comus*, VII, 128
  corruption in, V, 123
  imagery of, V, 102–03; VII, 128,
    130–31, 132
  light in, V, 102
  pastoral in, V, 120
  and *The Reason of Church-
    Government*, V, 109
  and *Of Reformation*, V, 109
  regeneracy in, V, 103, 104, 107, 124
  Virgil's influence in, VII, 153–54
*An Epitaph on the Marchioness of
  Winchester*
  and *An Apology*, V, 111
  epithalamic elements in, V, 41
  occasion of, III, 218
  regeneracy in, V, 103
Epithalamia
  in *L'Allegro*, V, 41
  biblical, XII, 30
  of Catullus, V, 40, 41, 42–47, 52,
    53, 54, 57
  in *Elegy 5*, V, 41
  in *An Epitaph on the Marchioness
    of Winchester*, V, 41
  nature in, V, 53–54
  in *PL*, V, 39–66
  pastoral in, V, 44, 54
  tradition of, V, 40–41, 47–49

Erasmus, Desiderius, VI, 200, 202–
  04; X, 103; XII, 52–53
  —*Adages*, XII, 202
  —*Novum Testamentum*, VI, 203
  —*Ratio seu Methodus Compendio
    Perveniendi ad Veram Theo-
    logiam*, VI, 202–03
  —*Responsio ad Disputationem
    cujusdam Phimostomi de
    Divortio*, VI, 203
Erdman, David, on Blake, XI, 56–59
Erikson, Erik, II, 180; VII, 63
Eros, I, 162, 163; IX, 39
Eschatology, Milton's, VIII, 165–207
Esdras, VII, 214
Estienne, Charles, I, 74
"Et Cetera Oath," VIII, 53
Eternal torment
  in *De Doctrina Christiana*, VIII,
    165–66, 190–202
  in Milton's early poetry, VIII,
    207n76
  in *PL*, VIII, 166–207
Eternity, in *PL*, XII, 76, 85–86, 87–
  88. *See also* Time
Ethos, I, 77–78
  in epic theory, I, 70–71, 72–73
  in *PL*, I, 76
  in Plato, VI, 217
Euripides
  and *Areopagitica*, IV, 112
  heroism in, VI, 244–45, 254
  Milton's admiration of, VI, 257–
    58n9
  and *SA*, VI, 248–57
  and *Sonnet 23*, X, 11–12, 116–19,
    121, 124, 128–29
  —*Alcestis*, X, 11–12, 116–19, 121,
    124, 128–29
  —*The Bacchae*, X, 13–14
  —*The Cyclops*, X, 7, 11
  —*Helen*, X, 12–13
  —*Heracles*, VI, 244–45, 246, 247,
    248–57; X, 14, 117

Euripides *(cont.)*
—*The Heraclidae*, X, 12
—*Iphigenia in Tauris*, X, 12–13
—*The Suppliants*, IV, 112
—*The Trojan Women*, I, 128–29
Eusebius, VII, 216; IX, 226
Evans, John Martin, V, 196–97; VII, 234
Evans, John X., on *Areopagitica*, IX, 169, 170, 185–86
Eve
and accommodation, VI, 94–95, 97
ambiguity of, XII, 20
and Chaos, XII, 11–12, 20
as child, IV, 15–16
and Christ, IV, 185–86; V, 143; VI, 19; IX, 141–42
as Circe, VI, 58–59, 60–65
creation of, V, 240–41; VII, 270–71; X, 117
and Death, VII, 298
as deviant, IX, 19–21
dream of, V, 233, 234–36, 237; XII, 25–45
duplicity of, IV, 12–13
education of, IV, 13–14; V, 243–45; X, 98
fall of, VIII, 240; IX, 87, 94–95; X, 101; XII, 6, 9, 83
and flowers, V, 160–62
in Gnostic writings, XII, 18–19
guilt of, XII, 9–10
innocence of, III, 120
intellect of, VI, 14–15
jealousy of, V, 219
and Lady Macbeth, V, 12
love lyric of, VI, 8; IX, 127–33
and Mary, VII, 268–69, 292–304, 305–06; XII, 19
as mother, IV, 8–10; IX, 17–18
and Narcissus, VII, 295, 299; IX, 16, 90–93; X, 97–98; XII, 12–14, 17–18
as part of Adam, XII, 20–21

as poet, VI, 8; IX, 19, 25
as revolutionary, V, 15; XII, 11
rhetoric of, VI, 8
and Satan, I, 103–07, 109, 110; V, 234–36; VI, 58–59; XII, 3–4, 10, 11, 12
self-knowledge of, III, 108–11, 113, 114, 115, 116–17
and Sin, IV, 11
soliloquy of, V, 215–18, 219
sonnets of, V, 140, 142–45
speech of, IV, 8–9; VIII, 255–56
as stereotype, IX, 21–22
temptation of, V, 214–15; VII, 300
as type of church, XII, 29–35
as wife, I, 136; VI, 9–10.
See also Adam and Eve
Evelyn, John, on gardens, V, 254, 255–56, 259, 262; VIII, 4, 14
Evening
in Catullus, VI, 265
contrasted with noon and midnight, VI, 267–68
in Fletcher, VI, 263
in *PL*, VI, 263–64, 265–73
in *PR*, VI, 273
in Spenser, VI, 262–63, 265
in Virgil, VI, 261–62
Everyman, in *PL*, V, 11, 15; VIII, 217–18, 219
Evil
in *Areopagitica*, III, 125; V, 8; XII, 37
and consciousness, XII, 10–22
in Dante, VI, 5
in *De Doctrina Christiana*, III, 125; VIII, 284–85
Dionysius on, I, 154
and imagination, V, 232–33, 235–36
knowledge of, III, 119–37; XII, 26–28
liveliness of, I, 26
in *Lycidas*, V, 123

origin of, I, 175
  in *PL*, I, 48, 93–94, 96, 108, 112–13; III, 119–37
  in pastoral, V, 22
  St. Augustine on, VIII, 283–84
  and selfhood, XII, 6, 10–22
  and sin, XII, 26–28
Exodus, Book of, II, 9–10
  Moses in, VII, 208, 210
  as source for *Lycidas*, IX, 223, 226
  as source for *PL*, II, 10–12; III, 166, 168, 170; IV, 209–10; VII, 213–14, 216–18
Exodus, myth of, II, 3–4
  in Bible, II, 6–7, 8
  and birth, II, 21–22
  and Fall of Man, II, 13–17
  and myth of return, II, 5–6
  in *PL*, II, 3–26
  in *PR*, II, 7
  in Plato, II, 9
  as recurring event, II, 18–19
  and resurrection, II, 19–21
  in *SA*, II, 7
Ezekiel, Book of
  Moses in, VII, 216
  as source for *PL*, III, 175–76, 178; IV, 212; VI, 108; IX, 52–55

Faculty psychology, III, 7; V, 231, 232–33, 237; XII, 26–27, 28, 39
Faith
  in *Comus*, VI, 122–23
  in *De Doctrina Christiana*, V, 203–04; VII, 238; IX, 245–46; X, 169, 170; XII, 69
  Manoa's lack of, II, 158–60, 198–202, 204
  in *PL*, VII, 238–39; IX, 122–23, 127, 134, 146
  St. Paul on, V, 71–72
  Samson's, XII, 129–30
  in *Sonnet 18*, X, 167–68, 170, 175
"Fall," in *PL*, VIII, 221–46

Fall
  of Adam, VI, 298; VIII, 240–41; IX, 87; X, 101–02; XII, 6, 83–84
  of Eve, VIII, 240; IX, 87, 94–95; X, 101; XII, 6, 9, 83
  of Satan, I, 47, 100–03; VII, 198–99; VIII, 229–35; IX, 87–88, 268; X, 65–66, 69–70
Fall of Man, II, 11–12
  in *Areopagitica*, XII, 28
  cause of, III, 122–23; XII, 3–24
  as continuing event, II, 213–14
  and Creation, XII, 4–5
  and Death, II, 53
  in *De Doctrina Christiana*, XII, 61
  Emerson on, XII, 5
  inevitability of, III, 134–35; V, 193
  myth of, IV, 5; VII, 244
  and myth of exodus, II, 13–17
  in *PL*, V, 19, 193–94, 213–28; IX, 14–15
  and parody, VII, 37
  in Pope, XI, 41
  results of, I, 137–39, 140, 143–44; II, 39, 52–54, 181, 211–12; III, 61, 84, 100, 126–27; IV, 12–17, 21, 34–36; V, 16, 62, 135, 156, 158, 159–60, 164, 166, 194, 198, 224; VI, 272, 300–01; VII, 219–21, 298; VIII, 24, 227, 229–30, 235, 241–42, 244–45, 248–51; IX, 142, 165; X, 95, 105, 106–07
  St. Augustine on, V, 197
  as spiritual death, VI, 187–88
  time of, IX, 82
Fallon, Robert Thomas, *XII, 165–95*
Fame
  and Clio, X, 40–45
  in *Lycidas*, III, 12–13; IV, 153–57
  in *SA*, X, 31
Family, in *Comus*, VI, 168–69, 170, 177. *See also* Kinship
Fancy. *See* Imagination

Fehl, Raina, II, 144
Felix culpa, I, 48, 175, 176, 177; II, 84; VII, 268; X, 105; XII, 25, 39
Fell, Kenneth, on *SA,* IV, 45
Fenner, Dudley, IX, 254, 255
Fenner, William
　—*The Souls Looking-Glasse,* III, 111–12
Ferry, Anne Davidson, VIII, 248
　on *PL,* X, 104–05, 107, 113; XII, 77
　on *SA,* XII, 127
Fescennine revelry, V, 44, 60–62
Fetish, VII, 251–53
Ficino, Marsilio
　—*De sole,* IX, 37–38
Fields, Albert W., III, 103, 132
Fiennes, Nathaniel, XII, 181, 183
Fink, Zera S., V, 272
Fire, I, 178–79, 181
　in *PL,* III, 56–57
　symbolism of, IX, 51–52
First Bishops' War, VIII, 54
First Defence. See *Defences*
Firth, Charles, IV, 53
Fisch, Harold, II, 15; IV, 196; VII, 213
Fish, Stanley E., *VII, 77–79;* VIII, 270
　on Dalila, X, 23
　on *PL,* II, 68; V, 221; IX, 89–101; XII, 6, 7
　on *PR,* VI, 222
　on *SA,* XII, 91, 118, 119–20
Fiske, Dixon, *VIII, 149–63*
"Five Arminian Articles," XII, 55–59
"Five Heads of Doctrine," XII, 55–56, 57–58
Fixler, Michael, *I, 167–92*
　on *PR,* I, 61; IV, 178
Fleming, Sir Oliver, XII, 169, 173
Flemming, W., III, 55–56
Fletcher, Giles, VII, 268
Fletcher, Harris Francis, I, 158; III,

187–88; VII, 102
　on *L'Allegro* and *Il Penseroso,* IX, 217
　on Milton's education, X, 178
　on *PL,* I, 152, 158; II, 16
　—*Milton's Rabbinical Readings,* IV, 195–215
Fletcher, John
　—*The Faithful Shepherdess,* V, 20–21
Fletcher, Phineas, VI, 263
　—*Apollyonists,* IV, 66
　—*Locustae,* IV, 66
　—*The Purple Island,* I, 26; IV, 80
Flowers
　in *Lycidas,* III, 15–17, 45, 63–65, 76; VIII, 11
　in *PL,* I, 160; II, 40–41; III, 75–76, 154; V, 156–62, 258–60; VII, 283; VIII, 11–12, 14–15
　in Spenser, III, 64.
　See also Landscape; Nature
"Fondly," in *Sonnet 19,* X, 142–43
Food
　and Communion, I, 140–43, 144
　in Genesis, I, 137
　in Levitical code, VII, 256–57
　in *PL,* I, 135–37, 139–40; II, 13; V, 167–68, 184, 187
　in *PR,* VII, 257; XII, 261–62
　in *SA,* II, 220–21
　as symbol of innocence, I, 140, 144.
　See also Fruit
Forgiveness
　in *PL,* X, 161–62
　in *Sonnet 19,* X, 162–63
Forsett, Edward
　—*A Comparative Discourse of the Bodies Natural and Politique,* IV, 80, 91, 94–95, 96
"Fortitude," in *De Doctrina Christiana,* VII, 292
Fortitude, civic
　in *Defences,* VIII, 90, 91–92

defined, VIII, 72
in *Tenure of Kings and Magis-
trates,* VIII, 87.
See also Heroism; Wisdom and
strength
Fortune, as goddess, XII, 202–04
Foster, Elizabeth, VIII, 150
Four, symbolism of, IX, 54–55, 269–
70
Four Daughters of God, VI, 125
Fowler, Alastair, on *PL,* V, 260; VI,
270–71; IX, 53, 154, 157, 159, 161
Foxe, John
—*Christus Triumphans,* VI, 119,
126–27, 129, 131, 133, 134
Fragrance, in Paradise, II, 41. *See
also* Air
Francini, Antonio, XII, 206–08
Franck, Sebastian
—*The forbidden fruit,* VII, 257
Fraser, Russell, VIII, 270
Fraud, in *PR,* IV, 181
Frazer, Sir James
—*Taboo and Perils of the Soul,*
VII, 259–60
Frederick Barbarossa, VI, 115
*A Free Commonwealth. See Readie
and Easie Way*
Free will
in Arminianism, XII, 56–59
in *Comus,* VI, 15–16
in *De Doctrina Christiana,* XII,
59–60
in Dryden, XI, 10
Erasmus on, XII, 52–53
Luther on, XII, 53
in *PL,* III, 104, 119–37; V, 18, 19;
IX, 137–39; XII, 49
in *PR,* VII, 202; IX, 263–64
St. Augustine on, XII, 50–52, 68
in *SA,* I, 132; VI, 255.
See also Choice, moral
Freud, Sigmund, VII, 129, 252; XII,
12

Friedman, Donald M., *III, 3–34*
Frith, John
—*Vox Piscis,* III, 112
Froschauer, Christopher, VII, 272
Frost, Gualter, Jr., XII, 173, 174,
184, 187
Frost, Gualter, Sr., XII, 172–73, 179
Frost, Joseph, XII, 170, 174, 184
Frost, Robert, I, 169
Fruit
in *PL,* III, 60, 152; IV, 155–56; V,
159–60, 165–71, 257, 258
of Tree of Knowledge, III, 60; V,
166, 167–68, 214–15, 216–18,
219, 222, 223–24
of Tree of Life, III, 60; V, 258
unhealthiness of, I, 137–38
Frye, Northrop, I, 178; XII, 20
on *Areopagitica,* IV, 110
on Bible, V, 23
on *Lycidas,* II, 125; III, 39; IX,
224
on myth, II, 6, 192; VI, 107
on *PL,* I, 45; II, 29, 43; VIII, 222,
281
on *PR,* I, 61; VI, 222
on *SA,* XII, 136
on tragedy, V, 11, 12, 13, 15, 16,
18, 19
Frye, Roland M., on *PL,* V, 224
Fulgentius the Mythographer, VIII,
74
on Clio, X, 42–43
on pastoral, III, 40, 42–43
Fulke, William, VI, 121
Fuller, Buckminster, VII, 38

Gabriel, and Satan, I, 42, 43; III, 106
Gafurius, on muses, X, 48
Galatians, Epistle to, VI, 233–34; X,
146
Gale, Theophilus, VIII, 249, 257
Galen, I, 137
Garden. *See* Gardens; Paradise

Gardening
  in *Animadversions,* V, 252
  in Paradise, V, 262–64
  in *Second Defence,* V, 252.
  See also Work
Gardens
  biblical descriptions of, V, 251
  English, V, 249–52, 259–60, 261,
    262; VIII, 4–25
  Milton's, V, 252, 259–60
  Oriental, VIII, 16, 21, 27
  as symbol of the soul, VII, 269–
    70.
  See also Landscape
Gardiner, Bishop, VI, 118
Gardner, Dame Helen
  on Donne, XI, 126
  on *PL,* II, 45; III, 159, 160; VIII,
    271, 279
  on tragedy, V, 9–10
Geddes, James, on Sophists, VI, 217
Gelli, Giovanni Battista
  —*Circe,* VI, 35–36, 55
Genesis, Book of, II, 10
  Creation in, VIII, 224
  food in, I, 137
  gardens in, V, 251
  imagination in, V, 232
  innocence in, III, 120–21, 122
  interpretation of, I, 154–55
  J text of, VII, 233–34
  marriage in, VI, 10, 208, 209
  as myth, VII, 234
  P text of, VII, 233–34
  St. Augustine on, VII, 269
  as source for *PL,* I, 152–53; III,
    165–66; IV, 205–08; V, 21, 167;
    VII, 101–25
  Spirit in, I, 149, 150
Geneva Bible, IV, 42; VII, 102, 107–
  08, 109, 110–11, 112–15, 116–17;
  XII, 30, 262
Genre, VII, 166
  Milton on, VII, 168–70

Gentil, Francis
  —*The Solitary or Carthusian
    Gard'ner,* V, 263
Geoffrey of Monmouth, IV, 127
Gerard, John, on English gardens, V,
  251, 252, 259, 262
Germany, in *Defences,* IV, 126–27
Getto, Giovanni, on Tasso, III, 84–
  85, 89
Giacomini, Lorenzo, II, 221
Giamatti, A. Bartlett, V, 54; X, 82, 88
  on *PL,* V, 230, 249
Giants
  in Book of Enoch, VIII, 187, 188–
    89
  in *PL,* VIII, 183–84, 185–86, 189
Gilbert, Allen H.
  on *PL,* V, 207
  on *SA,* XII, 91
Gilbert, Sir William, and Sullivan,
  Sir Arthur, VII, 7–8, 24
Gill, John, I, 17; IV, 144
Gilman, Wilbur, on *Areopagitica,* IX,
  177, 182
Gilpin, William S., VIII, 15, 16
Giorgione, Il, II, 47
  —*Tempest,* VIII, 31
Gluttony
  Milton on, II, 220–21
  in *PL,* IV, 185
  in *PR,* IV, 180, 181, 183, 185,
    186, 187, 189
Gnosticism, XII, 16, 18–19, 259
God
  in *An Apology,* V, 111–12
  authority of, IV, 23–25
  critical views of, VIII, 267–69;
    XII, 63
  in *De Doctrina Christiana,* III,
    160, 167–68; IV, 28; VII, 240
  Elohistic and Jahwistic, VII, 239–
    40
  eloquence of, VIII, 250, 252
  as father, IV, 7–8

as gardener, V, 262; VII, 270; XII, 32–33
in gunpowder poems, IV, 67, 69–71
in gunpowder sermons, IV, 65–66
irony of, IV, 69–72
and light, IX, 38, 159–60
in Old Testament, III, 161
in *PL*, III, 159–84; IV, 19–20, 23–24, 25–32, 33, 36–37, 69–72; VII, 240; VIII, 271–72
in *PR*, II, 89–90
reliability of, XII, 119, 121–25, 131–36
in *SA*, VII, 59–60
speech of, II, 89–90; IV, 25–29; VIII, 221–22
Gods, pagan. *See* Pagan gods
Godwin, Thomas
—*Moses and Aaron*, VII, 223
Goethe, Johann Wolfgang von, XI, 70
Goldberg, Jonathan, V, *177–90*
Goodman, Godfrey
—*The Fall of Man*, VIII, 247, 249, 252–53, 255, 257, 260
Goodness, ontological, III, 93, 97, 100
Gordon, Thomas, translation of Tacitus by, IV, 135
Gorgon, VII, 243; IX, 48, 49, 63–64
Gossman, A., II, 151
Gouge, William, IV, 47, 49; XII, 32, 33, 34
Governayle of Helthe, I, 137
Grace, W. J., on *PL*, VIII, 286
Grace
Arminians on, XII, 56–59
in Calvinism, XII, 55
in *De Doctrina Christiana*, XII, 59–60, 61, 63
Erasmus on, XII, 52–53
and imagination, V, 172, 174
and nature, V, 121
in *PL*, XII, 49, 64–69

resistible and irresistible, XII, 55–59
St. Augustine on, XII, 50–52, 68
Grant, John E., on Blake, VIII, 124, 132, 146nn19, 24
"Grateful," in *PL*, VI, 275n43
Gratitude, I, 98–100
Graves, Robert, on *L'Allegro*, VII, 83–84
Gray, Francis
—*The Judge's Scripture*, IV, 80
Greene, Robert, XII, 204
Greene, T. H.
on epic, I, 45–46
on *PL*, II, 41; V, 54; XII, 48–49
Greene, T. M., III, 167
Greenfield, Stanley, on *PL*, II, 30
Gregory, E. R., X, *35–64*
Gregory of Nyssa, St., VI, 279; XII, 260
Gregory the Great
—*Moralia*, VII, 304
Griffin, Dustin H., VI, *259–76; IX, 151–67*
Grose, Christopher, VII, *49–76*
Grosseteste, Robert, Bishop of Lincoln
on Moses, IX, 228, 229
—*Le Chasteau d'Amour*, VI, 125
Grotius, Hugo, VIII, 197
as source of rule of charity, VI, 205–06
—*Adamus Exul*, VI, 279
Guild, William
—*Moses Unvailed*, VII, 223, 224, 225, 228
Guillaume de Lorris
—*Roman de la Rose*, VII, 293, 295; XII, 223
Guimarães, Joao de, XII, 170
Gundolf, Friedrich, on dialogue, VI, 216
Gunpowder conspiracy, IV, 63–66
as influence on Milton, IV, 67–76

Gyfford, George, XII, 33–34
Gyraldus
—*De Musis Syntagma*, X, 43

Haemony, IV, 156–57; V, 96, 298–
99; VI, 174, 177; IX, 65–66
Haggai, as source for *Lycidas*, IX,
222–23, 227, 233
"Hail wedded Love," IV, 9–10, 11;
V, 46–47, 55–59; VI, 284–86
Hales, John W., on *Areopagitica*, IV,
101
Halkett, John, VIII, 248
Hall, Joseph, VII, 51; XII, 173
—*Defence of the Humble
Remonstrance*, VIII, 108
—*Episcopacie by Divine Right*,
IV, 87–88.
See also *Animadversions*
Haller, William, IV, 43, 45; X, 210
Halpert, V. B., on *L'Allegro*, VII, 80
Hamilton, K. G., V, 273; IX, 177
Hamilton, Sir Rostrevor, on *PL*, VIII,
267–68, 279–80, 280–81
Hamilton, W. Douglas, XII, 166
Hamlet, Desmond M., *VIII, 267–91*
Hammersmith and Horton
garden of, V, 252
Milton at, VII, 145–47; VIII, 42–
43, 44, 46–47, 50–51, 53, 57;
X, 151
Hanford, James Holly, IX, 233–34
on *Comus*, III, 69
on *PL*, VII, 208
on *SA*, II, 221; IV, 44, 59
Hanging Garden of Babylon, X, 81–
84
Harada, Jun, V, *213–28*
on *PL*, X, 104
Harapha (*SA*), I, 130; II, 164–66,
189–90; X, 14
as feudal soldier, IV, 52–53
limited vision of, XII, 156–57
and Lycus (*Heracles*), VI, 253–54

Harbage, Alfred, on tragedy, V, 8–9
Harding, Davis
on heroism, I, 41
on *PL*, I, 31–32; III, 168
Hardison, O. B., Jr., *I, 147–65;*
I, 16; V, 48; X, 44
Hardy, John E.
on *L'Allegro*, VII, 81
on Nativity ode, II, 107
Harington, Sir John, translation of
Orlando Furioso by, VI, 37
Harris, William O., on *SA*, XII, 93–94
Hartlib, Samuel, IX, 204, 206; XI,
74; XII, 174, 185
Hartmann, Geoffrey, V, 162
on *PL*, X, 101
Harvest, in *PL*, V, 171–72
Harvey, Gabriel, on education, IX,
205
Häublein, Ernst, *VII, 101–25*
Haug, Ralph M., on *The Reason of
Church-Government*, VIII, 53
Havens, Raymond Dexter, XI, vii, 29
Hawkins, Henry
—*Partheneia Sacra*, VII, 292–93,
295, 300
Hawkins, Sherman H., *II, 211–30*
Hawthorne, Nathaniel, and use of
multiple choice, VI, 109
Hayley, William, VIII, 128; XI, 69
Hayman, Francis, portrait of Milton
by, VIII, 145–46n14
Hayward, Sir John
—*Lives of the Three Normans*, IV,
137
Hazlitt, William
on Satan, XI, 85, 86
on Wordsworth, XI, 83
Head, symbolism of, IX, 56–58
Heaven
landscape of, II, 49–51; VIII, 33–
36, 37
and Paradise, V, 196
size of, II, 50–51

Hebrews, Epistle to. *See* Paul, St.

Hegel, G. W. F., IX, 61–62

Heinzelman, Kurt, *X, 111–25*

Hell
in Book of Enoch, VIII, 187
in *Comus*, VI, 148
in *De Doctrina Christiana*, VIII, 171–72
as Fascist state, V, 12
landscape of, II, 51–52; VIII, 33–36
after Last Judgment, VIII, 167–76
light in, III, 75
location of, VIII, 171–72, 174–76
in *In Quintum Novembris*, IV, 66

Heraclitus, IX, 54

Herbert, George, VII, 270, 279, 280; IX, 272
—"Affliction," I, 100
—"The Sacrifice," V, 183
—"Sunday," V, 180
—"Vanity (I)," X, 99

Hercules
and Christ, VI, 184–85; VIII, 156
in *Colasterion*, VIII, 85
in *First Defence*, XII, 244
in Harington, VI, 37
in Nativity ode, IV, 174
in *PL*, II, 32–33
in *PR*, XII, 242–45
and Samson, VI, 243–58
in Sandys, VI, 36–37
in seventeenth-century drama, VI, 244
in *Sonnet 23*, V, 76, 77; VI, 184–85.
See also Euripides; Sophocles

Heresbachius, on gardening, V, 262

Herford, C. H., on masque, VI, 144

Hermes, II, 12, 14; IX, 42, 56–57, 62
in *Comus*, VI, 133
in Homer, VI, 24

Hermes Trismegistus
—*Poimander*, I, 158

Herodotus, X, 85

Heroic drama, I, 55–56, 58–60, 62

Heroism
Abdiel's, II, 212
chivalric, II, 157; IX, 106–09
domestic, IX, 106, 115–18
in Euripides, VI, 244–45, 254
in history plays, V, 27–28
Milton on, I, 89–90
in Milton's blank-verse sonnets, V, 131–32
in Milton's prose, VIII, 71–101
and oratory, I, 74–75
in *PL*, I, 9–10; IV, 20; VIII, 183–86, 189; IX, 109–10, 115–18; XII, 48–49, 68–69, 84
parody of, VII, 40
in *SA*, III, 195–96; V, 131; VI, 255–57; VII, 45, 46, 69
Satan's perversion of, I, 41–43, 56–58, 71–72, 73–75; II, 60; V, 9–10; VIII, 184–86, 189; IX, 8
in *Sonnet 23*, X, 113–14
Son's, I, 43–44; II, 85, 90; V, 23–24, 25, 27, 28; VI, 106; IX, 8
in Sophocles, VI, 244–45
in *At a Vacation Exercise*, VIII, 52
in Virgil, I, 38–41, 46–47.
See also Wisdom and strength

Herrick, Marvin T., on Renaissance drama, V, 20, 21, 23, 24–25

Herrick, Robert
color use of, III, 72
—*Hesperides*, VI, 267
—*To the Virgins*, VI, 49–50

Herron, Dale, on *Sonnet 19*, X, 144

Hesiod
and War in Heaven, III, 171
—*Theogony*, I, 151–52; X, 37, 39

Hesperides
in *Comus*, IX, 48
in *PL*, VII, 249

Hesperus, in *PL*, V, 42–43; VI, 264–65, 270–71; IX, 152, 153

Hesse, Hermann
—*Steppenwolf*, VIII, 216–17
Heywood, Thomas, on pastoral, V, 22
Hierarchy
  in Milton, VI, 61–63; IX, 8–10,
    12–13; XI, 39
  in *PL*, IV, 21, 22; V, 166–67, 179–
    82, 187; VI, 6, 8; IX, 15–24,
    123–27; X, 96; XII, 3
  in Pope, XI, 39
  in *SA*, IX, 28–33.
  See also Authority
Hill, Christopher, XII, 62, 136
  on Milton's career as public
    servant, XII, 195n94
  on Puritanism, IV, 43–44, 45, 55,
    56
Hill, John Spencer, *II, 149–74; VIII,
  41–69; X, 127–39*
Hill, Thomas, on gardens, V, 255
Hills, in Paradise, II, 50, 75–78; V,
  254–55; VIII, 5–7, 21–22; X, 78,
  80–84
History
  in *An Apology*, II, 138
  in *Areopagitica*, IX, 173–74, 176
  Bible as, XII, 238–39, 250
  as branch of literature, II, 131–33
  in *De Doctrina Christiana*, V, 203
  Milton on, II, 131–48; XII, 240
  muse of, X, 40–42
  in *PL*, I, 62; V, 182–83, 185–87,
    191–92; XII, 87–88
  as precedent, IV, 122
  in *Prolusion 3*, II, 132
  in *Readie and Easie Way*, V, 279–
    80
  in *The Reason of Church-
    Government*, II, 132–33, 144
  Renaissance conceptions of, V, 24
  and rhetoric, II, 133–35, 137, 138–
    39, 140, 141, 143–44
  in *SA*, XII, 122, 124–25.
  See also Time

The History of Britain, II, 141–43,
  144–45; VII, 248, 260; X, 40
  astrology in, XII, 215
  Scripture in, XII, 238
  Tacitus' influence in, IV, 127–29,
    133, 134–36, 137
History play, V, 23–29
Hoard, Samuel, XII, 54
Hobbes, Thomas
  eschatology of, VIII, 199
  on *Second Defence*, V, 270
  —*An Answer to Bishop Bramhall*,
    VIII, 199
  —"Answer to Davenant's Preface
    to Gondibert," IX, 107–08
  —*Leviathan*, VIII, 199
Hoffman, Nancy Y., *II, 195–210*
Holinshed, Raphael, IV, 132–33,
  133–34
Hollander, John, V, 24
Holy Family, parodied in Nativity
  ode, IV, 172–73
Holy Spirit. *See* Spirit
Homer
  Arnold on, XI, 109
  Circe in, VI, 22–26
  color in, III, 56, 57, 68, 69
  comedy in, X, 5–6
  as influence on Milton, XI, 45
  landscape in, V, 253
  muse of, III, 27
  in *Second Defence*, VIII, 91–92
  as source for *L'Allegro* and *Il
    Penseroso*, IX, 210
  —*Iliad*, I, 39, 46; III, 68, 173; VI,
    5; VIII, 74, 81; IX, 153; X, 5–6
  —*Odyssey*, I, 38, 46, 74, 129; II,
    39; VI, 22–26; VIII, 74, 81; IX,
    56–57, 210; X, 5
Homeric Hymns, VII, 173, 174, 176,
  179
Homosexuality, VII, 127–63
Hone, Ralph, on *Lycidas*, IX, 223–24
Honigmann, E. A. J., X, 170

Hooker, Richard
—*Laws of Ecclesiastical Polity*,
IV, 81, 82, 85, 86, 87, 89; VII,
238
Hoole, Charles
—*New Discovery of the Old Art
of Teaching School*, X, 38
Hope
and despair, I, 80, 82–83, 85, 86
Manoa's, II, 203–04, 205–06
Horace, X, 52
—*Art of Poetrie*, X, 10
—*Carmen Sacculare*, VII, 174
Horse Chamber committee, XII,
170–71
Hortus conclusus, in Song of Solo-
mon, II, 22; VII, 130; XII, 30,
34–35
L'Hortus Deliciarum, VII, 276, 278,
281, 298
Hospitality
in Circean temptation, VI, 25, 27,
47, 66
in *PL*, I, 135–37, 139–40, 141–42
Hours of Catherine of Cleves, The,
VII, 272, 294
Howard, Donald R., on Milton's
career as public servant, XII, 178
Howard, Sir Robert, XI, 6
—*The Indian Queen*, I, 53, 55
Howat, G. M. D., XII, 182–83
"How soon hath Time the suttle
theef of youth." See *Sonnet 7*
Huckaby, Calvin, XI, 83
Hughes, Merritt Y.
on *L'Allegro* and *Il Penseroso*, IX,
203, 215
on Circe, VI, 22, 23
on *Doctrine and Discipline of
Divorce*, VI, 200
on *Epitaph on the Marchioness of
Winchester*, V, 41
on Milton's rhetoric, X, 179
on *PL*, I, 37; III, 163–64, 167, 179,

180; V, 5, 8, 178; VI, 296; VIII,
225, 285–86
on *PR*, VI, 216
on *Ad Patrem*, X, 40
on *SA*, VI, 248; X, 23, 30
on *Sonnet 23*, IV, 146; VIII, 151
on Spenser, VI, 35
Hugo of St. Victor, VI, 124–25
Huguelet, Theodore L., *VI, 199–214*
Huizinga, J., III, 61
Hume, Patrick, on *PL*, II, 30; III,
163, 179; IV, 210; VI, 260, 267,
271; IX, 160, 161
Humility, in *PL*, VII, 268–69; X,
74–75
Humility *topos*, VII, 171–72
Hunter, William B., Jr., VI, 135
on *PL*, X, 57
on *PR*, XII, 259
Huntington Kitto Bible, VII, 300, 301
Huntley, John H., on *Sonnet 23*, VI,
194; VIII, 151
Hyginus
—*Astronomi de Mundi et Sphere*,
X, 50
—*Fabularum Liber*, X, 43
Hyman, Lawrence, *II, 103–12*
on *PL*, VIII, 267–69, 280, 282–83
on *PR*, VI, 222
Hymen, V, 41, 46–47
Hymns
catalogue convention in, VII, 180–
81
classical tradition of, VII, 174
classification of, VII, 179
literary, VII, 167–70, 175–77, 180–
81
liturgical, VII, 173–77
in Middle Ages, VII, 174–75
and odes, VII, 167, 168–70
Reformation developments in,
VII, 175
Renaissance adaptation of, VII,
180

Hymns (cont.)
    Spenser's, VII, 168, 173, 177, 180-
        81
Hypocrisy, Milton on, VI, 285

Ibn Ezra, Rabbi Abraham, IV, 196-
    97, 201–02, 210, 212, 213–14
Ibsen, Henrik
    —The Lady from the Sea, XII,
    - 11–12
I Ching, XII, 3
Iconography, III, 55–60, 61–67; VII,
    267–311
Icons, I, 57, 60
Idealism, Platonic, V. 69. See also
    Neoplatonism; Platonism
De Idea Platonica, V, 120
Identity, loss of, I, 35
Idleness
    as Circean temptation, VI, 25, 26,
        28–29, 30, 33, 37, 63, 65–66,
        70–72
    in PL, VII, 295
    Puritans on, IV, 43–44, 45–46
Illuminated manuscripts, madonna
    in, VI, 120
Illustration
    of Bible, VII, 272–73, 300, 301
    as criticism, VIII, 123–24.
    See also Blake, William
Il Penseroso. See under Penseroso
"Image," VIII, 225–27; IX, 124
Imagery
    of L'Allegro and Il Penseroso, VIII,
        13; IX, 212
    of Animadversions, V, 91, 92, 105–
        06; VIII, 112–13
    of An Apology, V, 90, 91, 106,
        110–11, 116–17
    animal, V, 100–01, 105, 116; VIII,
        116; IX, 199; XII, 98–99
    of antiprelatical tracts, I, 18–19;
        V, 91–94
    apocalyptic, V, 103; VIII, 112–13

of Arcades, V, 93–94, 122
of Areopagitica, VII, 36–37; IX,
    169–70, 179–82, 185–201
of chronology, XII, 75–76
of Colasterion, VIII, 116–17
commercial, V, 113
of Comus, V, 122
of Defences, IV, 59–60
dissociation of, V, 68
of De Doctrina Christiana, VII,
    280–81
of Epitaphium Damonis, V, 102–
    03; VII, 128, 130–31, 132
food, II, 220–21; V, 91, 100
gardening, V, 155–76; VII, 270–
    72, 275, 277–78, 280–81, 283,
    286–87, 297, 306; XII, 32–33
of Lycidas, II, 124–25, 126; V,
    98–101, 122–23
medical, II, 217–22, 225; V, 91,
    109–10, 116–17
military, IV, 47–50, 59–60, 66;
    VIII, 73, 74, 77, 81–82, 86, 87;
    IX, 194–96, 197–98; XII, 102
musical, V, 110
of Nativity ode, II, 105–06, 108–
    10; V, 92–93, 122; VIII, 77
natural, IX, 212
naval, V, 98–99, 105; X, 27; XII,
    99–100
of PL, V, 155–76; VII, 270–72,
    275, 277–78, 283, 286–87, 297,
    306; IX, 78, 80, 81, 82, 84
of Prolusion 6, V, 91, 100, 122
in Puritan sermons, IV, 47–48, 66
and rationalism, V, 68–69, 73–74
of The Reason of Church-
    Government, V, 109–10, 113
of Of Reformation, V, 104–05;
    VIII, 76–77
of SA, II, 181–82, 188–89, 220–22,
    225; IV, 48–50; VI, 249; XII,
    92, 98–100, 102
sexual, VII, 128, 130–32, 153, 154

of *Sonnet 18*, X, 168, 171–72, 173–74, 175
of *Sonnet 23*, VI, 183
and typology, V, 67–85
of *At a Vacation Exercise*, V, 92, 122
Imagination, V, 72–73, 82; X, 84;
XII, 27, 28
Blake on, VIII, 137
and evil, V, 232–33, 235–36
in Genesis, V, 232
and grace, V, 172, 174
in *Lycidas*, III, 19
in *PL*, V, 233–47
and reason, XII, 39
in *The Reason of Church-Government*, V, 233
and typology, V, 72
Imitation of Christ, VII, 191, 268, 280, 305
Immortality, of Samson, III, 194; VI, 256–57
Incarnation, III, 97
in Nativity ode, IV, 163–64
in *PL*, IX, 96–97
Incest, IV, 10; VI, 110; VII, 39; IX, 23–24
Inexpressibility *topos*, VII, 172
Ingrafting in Christ, in *De Doctrina Christiana*, IV, 154–55; VII, 280
Innocence, I, 140, 144
in Genesis, III, 120–21, 122
and ignorance, V, 218, 222; XII, 8, 28, 37
meaning of, III, 121–22
in *PL*, III, 116, 119–37
In Obitum Praesulis Eliensis. See under *Obitum*
In Quintum Novembris. See under *Quintum*
Insects, in *PL*, V, 165
Inspiration
biblical, I, 148
femaleness of, IV, 7.
See also Muses; *PL*, muse of

Intemperance, in Circe myth, VI, 31, 34, 35
Intention, authorial, VIII, 211–12
Intercourse. *See* Sexual intercourse
Interpreter's Bible, IX, 53, 54–55
Intuition, in criticism, VII, 6–8, 9–10
Inversion, in *Comus*, VII, 35–36
Investiture, IV, 85–88
Irony
in *An Apology*, V, 117
in *Areopagitica*, IV, 104–05, 109–11, 112
Christ's, V, 90
in *Colasterion*, VIII, 115
God's, IV, 69–72
in gunpowder poems, IV, 72–73
in *PL*, IV, 69–72, 73–75; V, 9, 32, 59–60, 246; VI, 105; VII, 286; VIII, 240; XII, 40
in *PR*, IV, 191; V, 78; VI, 235–36
in *Readie and Easie Way*, V, 284, 286
in *The Reason of Church-Government*, V, 87–88, 114–15
in *SA*, II, 169, 197, 198; V, 78; VII, 58; X, 15–16; XII, 108, 109, 159–60
in *Sonnet 23*, V, 75; VI, 192
in Tacitus, IV, 131, 132, 134, 138
Isaiah, Book of, V, 82
allusions to, in *PR*, VI, 236
and *An Apology*, V, 99–100
as source for *Lycidas*, IX, 238
as source for Nativity ode, IV, 171–72
as source for *PL*, III, 162, 177, 178, 180; IV, 211–12, 212–13
Tree of Jesse in, V, 183
Isocrates
—*Areopagiticus*, IV, 101, 102, 103, 105–09; IX, 188, 199–200
Italian poems, VII, 142–43
and *An Apology*, V, 110
dating of, VII, 143

Italian poems *(cont.)*
 love in, V, 120
 psychological content of, VII, 144–
  45
Ithuriel, III, 105, 106
Itzkoff, Seymour W., VI, 88

Jackson, J. L., on *Sonnet 19*, X, 144
Jacobus, Lee A., *III, 103–18*
 on *PL*, X, 97–98; XII, 13–14
James, Epistle of, as source for *PL*,
 VI, 110
James I, IV, 44, 92; XII, 60
James, D. G., on Keats, XI, 105
Jason, IX, 48
Jayne, Sears, VI, 167; VII, 180
 on *Comus*, IX, 65
Jealousy, in *PL*, V, 219
Jean, Duke of Berry
 —*Très Riches Heures*, VII, 279,
  299, 302; XII, 99
Jebb, Sir Richard, on *SA*, XII, 118
Jeremiah, and *Sonnet 23*, IV, 145–46
Jerome, St., I, 153; IX, 227; XII, 31
Jerusalem Talmud, Samson in, VI, 247
Jessop, William, XII, 184, 185
Jewish tradition
 and *PL*, IV, 195–215; XII, 17
 in *SA*, III, 185–200; IV, 199–200,
  202–05, 211; VI, 247
 in *Sonnet 23*, VI, 182, 185.
 See also Old Law
Joachim of Fiore, XI, 55, 66
Job, Book of, II, 180; X, 16
 as source for *PL*, IV, 205
 as source for *SA*, XII, 128–29,
  131–32
Joel, allusions to, in *PR*, VI, 235
John, St., Gospel of, V, 69, 98; VI,
 228–29; IX, 38
John Chrysostom, St.
 Milton's knowledge of, XII, 220
 —*Sixth Sermon on Matthew*, XII,
  218–19

John of Damascus
 —*Exposition of the Orthodox
  Faith*, IX, 53
John of Patmos. *See* John the Divine,
 St., Revelation of
John of Salisbury
 —*Policreticus*, IV, 81
John of the Cross, St., VII, 270
John the Divine, St., Revelation of,
 II, 212–13
 angels in, XI, 52, 53, 54, 56, 57,
  60–62, 66, 70, 72–73
 exodus in, II, 7, 8
 purification in, VI, 186; VIII, 152
 river of life in, II, 49
 as source for *Animadversions*, VI,
  114–15; VIII, 112–13
 as source for Blake's *Milton*, XI,
  55–56, 60–62, 65, 66, 70, 71,
  72–75
 as source for *Comus*, VI, 115
 as source for *De Doctrina
  Christiana*, VIII, 190–92
 as source for *Lycidas*, IX, 223,
  234, 238
 as source for mystery plays, VI,
  113, 115–16, 119, 134
 as source for *PL*, III, 171, 177,
  178; V, 198
 as source for *PR*, VI, 230, 231,
  235–36, 238–39
 as source for *Sonnet 23*, IV, 146,
  147; X, 135
 time in, II, 5
Johnson, Lee M., *V, 129–53*
Johnson, Samuel
 Arnold on, XI, 110
 on *Lycidas*, III, 38; IV, 152
 on Milton's sonnets, X, 137
 on Milton's theology, XII, 47
 on *PL*, V, 80; VI, 301; IX, 86, 151
 on *SA*, II, 149; V, 80, 81; VII, 49,
  50; XII, 91, 118
 on War in Heaven, X, 155

Johnson, S. F., on Hamlet, VII, 63
Jonathan Targum, III, 187, 188; IV,
    197, 198, 208, 211
Jones, Inigo, VI, 144, 145, 147
Jones, Nicholas R., *VIII, 221–46; X,
    167–76*
Jonson, Ben, V, 61–62; VIII, 247,
    250, 258
    court masques of, VI, 144, 146
    Milton on, IX, 213
    translation of Horace's *Art of
        Poetrie* by, X, 10
    —*Pleasure Reconciled to Virtue*,
        VI, 46
    —*Sejanus*, IV, 131
    —"To Sir Henrie Savile," IV, 130
Jordan, Richard Douglas, *IX, 261–75*
Josephus, Flavius, VII, 250, 252; X,
    82; XII, 258
    on Moses, VII, 209, 212, 214–15
    on Samson, III, 187
Joyce, James
    —*Portrait of the Artist*, II, 22
Jude, General Epistle of, as source
    for *PL*, VIII, 188–89
Judge, identity of, in *PL*, VI, 103–04
Judgement of Martin Bucer, VI, 203,
    204, 205
    heroism in, VIII, 84
    response to, X, 195
    use of authority in, X, 184–85
Judges, Book of
    rabbinical commentaries on, III,
        186–89
    Samson in, VI, 245, 246, 247, 256
    as source for *SA*, II, 220
Jung, C. G., IX, 69; XII, 5
    —*Symbols of Transformation*, IX,
        55, 56, 58, 59, 60
Justice
    divine, XII, 50–55, 56, 59–60, 61–70
    in *Lycidas*, II, 121–25
    in *PL*, III, 162, 163–66; IV, 24–25,
        29; VIII, 271, 272, 273–79

Kairos
    biblical use of, XII, 197–98
    defined, VII, 189–90, 191–92; XII,
        197
    in Milton's early poetry, XII, 199–
        200
    in Milton's prose, XII, 199
    and Occasio, XII, 202
    in Puritan theology, XII, 198
    statue of, XII, 197, 201–02.
    See also Time
Kantorowicz, Ernst H., IV, 81
Kastor, Frank S., on Nativity ode,
    VII, 178–79
Keats, John
    Arnold on, XI, 106, 107
    and Milton, XI, 99–105, 113
    on Shakespeare, XI, 99
    on Wordsworth, XI, 100
    —*Endymion*, VIII, 58; XI, 101
    —*The Fall of Hyperion*, XI, 103–
        05
    —*Hyperion*, XI, xii–xiii, 101
    —*Ode to Psyche*, XI, 102–03
    —*Sleep and Poetry*, XI, 102
Kelley, Maurice
    on *De Doctrina Christiana*, IX,
        255; XII, 63
    on *PL*, IX, 80–81; XII, 63
Kelsall, Malcolm, *XII, 235–51*
Kepler, Johann
    on astrology, XII, 216
    Milton's knowledge of, XII, 228
    on Star of Bethlehem, XII, 225–28
    —*De Stella Nova in Pede
        Serpentarii*, XII, 225–28
Kermode, Frank, VII, 108
    on pastoral, VIII, 35
Kessner, Carole S., *VI, 243–58*
Kierkegaard, Søren
    on dread, XII, 9–10
    on sin, XII, 7–9
Kimchi, Rabbi David, III, 187, 188;
    IV, 197–98

King, Edward, II, 122; III, 3; VIII, 48
Kings, First Book of, as source for
PL, III, 169–70
Kingsley, Lawrence W., IV, 163–76
on Nativity ode, VII, 174
Kinship
defined, IV, 6
in PL, IV, 6–11, 13, 17–18; IX, 15–24
in SA, IX, 28–33
Kirchmayer, Thomas
—Pammachius, VI, 116–19, 121,
129, 133
Klein, Jacob, on Socratic dialogue,
VI, 216, 217
Kluger, Rivkah Schärf, XII, 20
Knight, Douglas, XI, 29
Knight, G. Wilson, IX, 44–45
on Comus, IX, 65
on Pope, XI, 33
Knott, John R., Jr., II, 37–58
on PL, V, 250, 252
"Knowledge," in PL, III, 127–28
Knowledge
in Areopagitica, III, 132–33
Christ's, IX, 265–68
in Comus, V, 290
of evil, III, 119–37; XII, 26–28
of God, III, 160
and light, III, 30–31
in PL, II, 30–31, 119–37
in PR, VI, 220–21
Plato on, VI, 220
in Tasso, III, 94, 96–97.
See also Self-knowledge
Koehler, G. Stanley, III, 55–81;
VIII, 3–40
Kohn, Terry Kidner, VI, 143–64
Koldewey, Robert, X, 85–86
Kranidas, Thomas, I, 15–29; X, 185
on antiprelatical tracts, V, 125n4
on Dalila, X, 25–26, 27, 30
Kristeller, Paul Oscar, on rhetoric,
X, 178

Krouse, F. M., on SA, II, 162, 227–28; III, 198; IV, 40, 41; X, 24;
XII, 118
Kuhn, Thomas, VI, 87–89

La Boétie, Estienne de
—Discours de la servitude
volontaire, IV, 119
Labriola, Albert C., VII, vii–xii, 267–311
Lactantius
—De Ave Phoenice, VIII, 22
Lady (Comus)
emotions of, VI, 171–72
faith of, VI, 122–23
intellect of, VI, 15–17
lack of growth in, VI, 175–77
limitations of, V, 295, 296, 297,
300, 303
paralysis of, IX, 65
skills of, V, 295–96, 299–300,
301–02
social role of, IX, 26–27
soliloquy of, V, 295–96
view of wood of, VI, 152–53
as warfaring Christian, VII, 149
"Lady of Christ's," VII, 136–37
Lady Wandering in the Wilderness,
VI, 115–17, 119, 121, 124, 135–36
in Comus, VI, 120–21, 122–23,
124, 127–28
L'Allegro. See under Allegro
Lamb, Charles, XII, 261
Lamentations of Jeremiah, as source
for SA, XII, 128–29
Landor, Walter Savage, on PL, X,
159; XI, 83
Landscape
in L'Allegro, VII, 85; VIII, 10, 11,
12, 13
baroque, VIII, 11–12, 16, 19, 21,
27
bower in, VIII, 20–21
of Chaos, VIII, 36–37

in *Comus*, II, 38; VI, 143–64;
   VIII, 13–14
and contemplation, VIII, 28–29
of heaven, II, 49–51; VIII, 33–36,
   37
of hell, II, 51–52; VIII, 33–36
in Homer, V, 253
in *Lycidas*, VII, 11, 12
melancholy in, VIII, 6
and moral instruction, VIII, 4–5,
   27–29
in Nativity ode, VIII, 12
in paintings, II, 47
in *PL*, II, 37–58; V, 249–67; VIII,
   3–40
in *PR*, I, 61
in *Il Penseroso*, VIII, 13
picturesque in, VIII, 4–19
Renaissance style of, VIII, 11, 12–
   13, 25, 28, 32
sculpture in, VIII, 27
surprise in, VIII, 25–26
"terrible" in, VIII, 25–26
and time, VIII, 29
water in, VIII, 16–19.
   See also Flowers; Gardens;
   Nature; Trees
Landy, Marcia, *II, 175–94; IV, 3–18;
   IX, 3–36;* VI, 3–4
on Dalila, X, 26, 31
on *PL*, XII, 3
Langdon, Ida, I, 16
Language
   as aggression, II, 185
   corruption of, VIII, 248–57
   fallen and unfallen, II, 28–29, 32,
      33–34; VIII, 227, 248; X, 105–
      06
   God's, IV, 25–26, 29; V, 172–74;
      VIII, 221–22, 248–52; X, 157–58
   masculinity of, IV, 7
   Milton's view of, IX, 4
   in *PL*, II, 89–90; IV, 8–9, 25–29;
      V, 172–74; VI, 300–01; VIII,

221–22, 247–66; IX, 129–30,
   132; X, 104–06, 158
purification of, V, 225
and reality, II, 178, 184, 185,
   187, 191
in *SA*, II, 185–88
Satan's, IV, 25–26, 29; VIII, 254–
   55, 256; IX, 130–31; X, 158–59
in *Faerie Queene*, VIII, 250.
   See also Soliloquies
The Lanterne of Light, VI, 121–22
Lapide, Cornelius à, VII, 193–94
Lark, in *L'Allegro* and *Il Penseroso*,
   V, 74; VII, 78, 81; VIII, 134
Last Judgment
   in *De Doctrina Christiana*, VIII,
      169, 190–92
   in Nativity ode, II, 104, 109
   in *PL*, II, 23; VIII, 167–76
   in *Of Reformation*, I, 27–28
   in Tasso, III, 94, 97–98
Last Supper, and meal in Eden, I,
   142–43
"On the Late Massacre in Piemont."
   See *Sonnet 18*
Laud, Archbishop, VIII, 48, 197;
   XII, 47
—*Constitutions and Canons
   Ecclesiastical*, IV, 88; VIII, 53
Lavater, Johann Caspar, XI, 75–76
Law
   in antiprelatical tracts, XII, 142,
      143
   in *De Doctrina Christiana*, VII,
      235–37, 261; XII, 143–44
   in *Doctrine and Discipline of
      Divorce*, VII, 235
   and liberty, XII, 143–46, 154
   Milton on, XII, 142–46
   Mosaic, III, 187–98; XII, 154–55
   St. Paul on, XII, 142–43
   in *SA*, II, 186, 187; III, 187–98;
      XII, 150–53
   in *Tetrachordon*, VII, 237–60

Law *(cont.)*
in *A Treatise of Civil Power,* VII,
261.
See also New Dispensation; Old
Law
Lawes, Henry, III, 218; VI, 50
portrayed in *Comus,* V, 290, 291,
292, 296, 299, 303, 305–06
and production of *Comus,* VI, 167,
169
and publication of *Comus,* III,
203; VIII, 57–58, 61
Lawns, VIII, 12
Lawrence, Henry, XII, 183
Lawry, Jon S., V, 203; VIII, 272
Lawson, William
—*A New Orchard and Garden,* V,
254, 260
Leadership, in *PL,* VI, 13–14
Leavis, F. R., V, 67
on *PL,* I, 2; II, 38
Le Comte, Edward, *XII, 253–66*
on *Comus,* IV, 157
on *Sonnet 23,* VI, 189; VIII, 159,
161
Lee, Nathaniel, XI, 9–10
Lee, Edward
—*Critica sacra,* VII, 193, 259
—*A Treatise of Divine Promises,*
VII, 235
Leighton, Alexander
—*An Appeal to the Parliament,*
IV, 95–96
Leisegang, Hans, IX, 50
Leishman, J. B.
on *L'Allegro,* VII, 83
on Nativity ode, VII, 168
Le Nôtre, André, VIII, 35, 36
The Letany of John Bastwick, IV, 87
Lethe, VIII, 34
"Letter to a Friend," VII, 146–47
Milton's vocational choice in, III,
23–24; VIII, 44, 46–47, 50
pragmatism in, V, 273

and *Readie and Easie Way,* V,
277–78
Levellers, X, 210–11
Lévi-Strauss, Claude, IV, 5, 6
Levitical code
cursed foods in, VII, 256–57
irrationality of, VII, 260–61
Leviticus, Book of
purification in, VI, 185–86; VIII,
152
as source for *PL,* IV, 213–14; VII,
258
as source for *PR,* VII, 257
as source for *Sonnet 23,* V, 75
Lewalski, Barbara K., *VI, 3–20; XI,
29–50;* IX, 3–4, 11, 12, 18
on *PL,* VI, 299; VII, 227; IX, 125;
XII, 76
on *PR,* I, 52; II, 96; IV, 178; VI,
224; VII, 42–43; IX, 262, 263,
269; XI, 12; XII, 254
on *Readie and Easie Way,* V, 272
Lewis, C. S., VII, 242
on epic, I, 48
on *PL,* I, 2, 93, 139, 149; II, 38;
IV, 20; VI, 277
on *PR,* I, 46
L'Hortus Deliciarum, VII, 276, 278,
281, 298
Liberty
in antiprelatical tracts, XII, 142
in *Areopagitica,* IV, 105–06, 108
and Circe, VI, 54–58
and education, IV, 106
and law, XII, 143–46, 154
and moral choice, IV, 108
in *PL,* III, 197; VIII, 286–87; XII,
6–7
in *Readie and Easie Way,* V, 282–
83, 284–85
in *Of Reformation,* V, 270
in *SA,* III, 193–94, 196, 197–98;
XII, 141
in *Second Defence,* V, 269–70

and sin, XII, 8–9
  in Tacitus, IV, 118–19, 125–26.
  See also Choice, moral
Lieb, Michael, *IV, 79–99; VII, vii–xii, 233–65*
  on *PL,* VI, 6; IX, 66–67
Life of Christ, IX, 273
Light
  in *Animadversions,* V, 111; VIII, 113
  in antiprelatical tracts, V, 100
  in *An Apology,* V, 110–11
  in Blake's illustrations for *L'Allegro* and *Il Penseroso,* VIII, 134, 135–36, 142
  in *Comus,* VI, 155–56; VII, 34
  in *Epitaphium Damonis,* V, 102
  of God and Christ, IX, 38, 159–61
  in *Heracles,* VI, 249
  in hell, III, 75
  and knowledge, III, 30–31
  and Logos, IX, 38–39
  in Nativity ode, II, 105–06, 108, 110; IV, 164–65, 168
  in *PL,* II, 64–68, 80; III, 61, 68–69, 70, 72–77, 100, 168, 176–77; V, 31–32; VI, 105; VII, 216–18; VIII, 5–6, 35, 37–38; IX, 82; XII, 187
  in *PR,* II, 94, 95, 97
  in *Il Penseroso,* III, 73; VII, 87–88, 92
  Platonist view of, IX, 37–38
  in *SA,* II, 176–78, 193; VI, 249
  in *Sonnet 23,* IV, 147
  in Tasso, III, 85–100.
  See also Blindness
Likeliest Means to Remove Hirelings, IV, 93; VIII, 55, 158; X, 182, 185
Lilburne, John, VIII, 48
Lindenbaum, Peter, *VI, 277–306*
Linocre, G.
  —*Musarum Libellum,* X, 37, 43
Lipsius, IV, 117, 125

Litotes, in *Sonnet 18,* X, 173
Little Non-Such, X, 197
Littleton, Adam, on Clio, X, 44
Liturgy, I, 172–73
  kairos and *chronos* in, VII, 192–93
  Milton on, IV, 88
Livy, XII, 239
  —*Historiarum . . . Libri,* IV, 94
Lloyd, Michael, on *Lycidas,* III, 20
Locus amoenus, III, 15–16; VII, 293–96; VIII, 3
Logic, in Marprelate, VIII, 105. See also *Art of Logic*
Logos
  and light, IX, 38–39
  masculinity of, IX, 39
  nature of, IX, 54
Long, Anne B., *VI, 85–99*
Longinus
  on rhetoric, X, 180
  —*On the Sublime,* X, 180
Long Parliament, V, 108, 110–12, 117, 124, 271, 272; VII, 50–52; XII, 186
Lorens d'Orléans, Friar
  —*Somme le Roi,* VII, 269–70
Lorraine, Claude, VIII, 6
Love
  angelic, VI, 296–97
  in Milton's Italian poems, V, 120
  in *PL,* III, 65–66; IV, 29–32, 34–36; V, 21, 222–25; VI, 191–92, 266, 268–69; VIII, 23–25
  in *SA,* VI, 255
  Satan's, I, 103–04, 105
  in *Sonnet 23,* VI, 183, 189–92
  in Tasso, VI, 28–31
Lovejoy, Arthur, on *PL,* X, 99–100, 103
Low, Anthony, *I, 135–45; IV, 19–38*
  on *SA,* XII, 94, 118, 127
Lowell, Robert
  version of *Prometheus Bound* by, X, 8

Lucian
—*How to Write History*, II, 139–
    40, 143
Lucifer, in Nativity ode, IV, 169, 174
Lucretius
—*De Rerum Natura*, I, 152, 161
Ludolphus de Saxonia
—*Vita Jesu Christi*, IX, 270
Ludus de Antichristo, VI, 115–16,
    129, 133
Luke, St., Gospel of
    as source for *PL*, VIII, 189; XII, 41
    as source for *PR*, VI, 235, 239;
        VII, 196; IX, 268
    as source for *SA*, I, 118
    as source for *Sonnet 23*, V, 75
Lustratio, II, 216–17, 218, 219, 226–
    27
Luther, Martin, VI, 129–30
    on Adam and Christ, IX, 262
    on astrology, XII, 225
    on free will, XII, 53
    on St. Paul's affliction, X, 145–46
    on sexual intercourse, VI, 281
—*The Gospel for the Festival of
        the Epiphany*, XII, 225
—*Lectures on Genesis*, VII, 254
Lycidas, VII, 153; IX, 106
    Alpheus in, III, 15, 50
    ambiguity in, II, 119–20, 124,
        126–27
    and antiprelatical tracts, V, 98–
        102, 104–05, 109, 110, 119
    Apollo in, III, 37
    astrology in, XII, 214
    Atropos in, II, 124–25, 126
    biblical sources of, IX, 222–23,
        225–27, 233, 234, 235–36, 238
    blindness in, II, 124–25
    Camus in, III, 14, 37
    canzoni of, V, 129
    catalogue in, III, 15–16, 63–65
    as catharsis, VIII, 53
    Christ in, III, 44; IV, 155; V, 77;

        IX, 43, 223–24
    Circe in, VI, 39
    coda of, III, 8, 13, 25–26
    color in, III, 57, 62, 63–65, 68, 70
    commiato of, III, 35–36, 38, 51
    conflict in, III, 5
    contemplation in, III, 42
    corruption in, V, 88
    death in, IV, 157–58
    and Dryden's "Ode on the Death
        of Mr. Henry Purcell," XI, 14–16
    education in, III, 3–34
    evil in, V, 123
    as expression of unreadiness, VIII,
        59–60
    fame in, III, 12–13; IV, 153–57
    flowers in, III, 15–17, 45, 63–65,
        76; VIII, 11
    imagery of, II, 124–25, 126; V,
        98–101, 122–23
    imagination in, III, 19
    justice in, II, 121–25
    and Keats's *Ode to Psyche*, XI, 103
    landscape in, VIII, 11, 12
    locus amoenus in, III, 15–16
    magic in, III, 42
    metaphor in, III, 21–22
    Milton's vocational choice in, III,
        11–12, 21–23; VIII, 47–51
    Moses in, IX, 225–34, 237
    muses in, II, 121–22; X, 38–39
    music in, IV, 159–60
    myth in, VI, 108
    nature in, V, 101
    Neoplatonism in, III, 38–39
    occasion of, III, 3–4
    Orpheus in, II, 53; III, 11, 38–39;
        V, 74, 77; IX, 42–43; XI, 15
    pastoral in, III, 5, 9, 11–20, 22,
        26, 36, 39–40, 41–45, 47–51;
        IV, 152–53; V, 77, 98, 120
    pathetic fallacy in, III, 10
    persona of, III, 5–6, 35–36, 37
    phallic symbolism in, VII, 153

Phoebus in, III, 13, 48; IV, 151–52, 153, 155, 157–59; V, 77; IX, 237, 238–39

plants in, III, 7–9, 13, 38, 39, 41, 44–45; IV, 153–54, 156–57

and Pope's *Epilogue to the Satires,* XI, 36

and Pope's *Pastorals,* XI, 32

and *Of Prelatical Episcopacy,* V, 102

priesthood in, III, 42

prophecy in, III, 43

and *The Reason of Church-Government,* V, 99, 101

and *Of Reformation,* V, 98, 99, 100, 104–05, 109

regeneracy in, V, 102, 103, 107, 112, 124

St. Michael in, III, 18

St. Peter in, II, 123–24, 125–26; III, 14–17, 20, 37, 42, 43, 44, 47, 48–50; IV, 152; V, 77; IX, 223–24, 234–35, 237

self-education in, III, 3–34

and Shelley's *Adonais,* XI, x–xi

"shepherd" in, III, 14–17, 32

Sicilian Muse in, III, 15, 50; IV, 153; IX, 238–39

"smite" in, II, 125

solar symbolism in, IX, 42–43, 44

soliloquy in, VII, 72

sound in, III, 9–11, 15

Spenser's influence in, IX, 229–30

star in, XII, 230

structure of, II, 121–22; III, 39–40, 45; V, 146; IX, 236–37

style of, III, 45, 46, 47–51

subject of, XI, xiii

syntax of, III, 17

Tacitus' influence in, IV, 120, 125

tenses in, IV, 157–59

time in, III, 13, 26; IV, 159

truth in, III, 18–19, 25–26

typology in, V, 74, 77; IX, 224

water in, VIII, 16–17.

See also "Two-handed engine"

Lydgate, John

—*Pilgrimage of the Life of Man,* IX, 229

Lydian airs, in *L'Allegro,* VII, 86–87; IX, 217

Lyons, Bridget, on *Il Penseroso,* VII, 94

Lysippus, XII, 201

McAdams, James R., *IV, 177–93*

Macaulay, Thomas, XI, 110

MacCaffrey, Isabel, on *PL,* II, 68; VII, 216; VIII, 278; IX, 78–88, 127; XII, 77

McColley, Diane, *XII, 25–45*

McColley, Grant, on *PL,* VIII, 186

McCown, Gary M., *V, 39–66*

McDill, Joseph M., on *PL,* XII, 48

Machiavelli, Niccolò, II, 143; IV, 118

Mack, Maynard, on Pope and Milton, XI, 29, 38–39

MacKellar, Walter

on *Ad Patrem,* X, 40

on *PR,* XII, 255, 257

Macrobius, X, 38, XII, 17

Macropedius

—*Adamus,* V, 20

Maddison, Carol, on Nativity ode, VII, 167

Madonna, representations of, VI, 120–21. *See also* Mary

Madsen, William, III, 96; V, 69, 70

on *Comus,* VI, 52

on *PL,* II, 177; VII, 210, 221; X, 95

on *PR,* I, 61

Magi, XII, 217–22, 225–30

Magic

in *Comus,* VI, 174

in *Lycidas,* III, 42

St. Augustine on, X, 105

Magnanimity, Milton on, I, 189–90*n16*

Magus, Simon, XII, 16

Mahood, M. M., on *PL*, III, 150

Maimonides, Moses
on Samson, III, 189
—*Guide of the Perplexed*, VII, 260–61

Major, John, on Milton's rhetoric, X, 178

Malachi, allusions to, in *PR*, VI, 236

Male, Emile, V, 183

Malvezzi, Vergilio, IV, 120, 121, 122

Mammon, V, 14

Mandeville, John, VII, 252

Mankind, VI, 125

Manoa, I, 122–25, 131–32; II, 195–210; VII, 65–66
and Adam, II, 209
and Amphitryon, VI, 249–50
and Belial, II, 202
biblical account of, II, 196, 205
blindness of, X, 15
comic element in, X, 14–16
education of, II, 169–70, 171, 207–09
hope of, II, 203–04, 205–06
lack of faith of, II, 158–60, 198–202, 204
language of, II, 185–86
Samson's rejection of, II, 198
sonnets of, V, 149
as tempter, IV, 41–42; VI, 71–72, 73; VII, 55

Manso, John Baptisto, Marquis of, VIII, 62; X, 45

Mansus
and *An Apology*, V, 111, 119
Clio in, X, 36, 45
color in, III, 60, 68
epic projected in, VIII, 64, 72
regeneracy in, V, 107, 124

Mantuan
—*Adolescentiae*, III, 37

Marcuse, Herbert, XII, 12–13, 14

Marilla, E. L., XII, 255

Mark, St., Gospel of
as source for *PL*, VIII, 169–70
as source for *PR*, VI, 239
as source for *SA*, V, 79

Markham, Gervase
—*The English Housewife*, V, 252, 263

Marprelate, Martin
influence of, VIII, 106–19
rhetorical style of, VIII, 104–06

Marriage
in *Book of Common Prayer*, VI, 302n1
in Circe myth, VI, 24–25, 31, 47–48, 61–63
in *De Doctrina Christiana*, V, 55; VII, 277
in *Doctrine and Discipline of Divorce*, VI, 10–11
in Genesis, VI, 10, 208, 209
hierarchical, VI, 61–63
as companionship, VI, 6, 9–10
in *PL*, IV, 9–11, 14–17; VI, 61–64; VII, 273–78; VIII, 258; IX, 110–11, 114–15
patriarchal, VI, 73
Protestant theologians on, VI, 281–83
Reformers on, XII, 33–34
Renaissance concept of, VI, 78n19
St. Paul on, VI, 281–82, 287
in *SA*, I, 119–20, 123; II, 154–55, 200; X, 25, 30; XII, 106–07, 150–53, 155–56
in *Sonnet 23*, IV, 146, 147.
See also Divorce; Divorce tracts; Epithalamia

Marriage couch, in epithalamic tradition, V, 54–55

Marriage god, in *PL*, V, 46–47

Marriage torch, in *PL*, V, 43

Marshall, Stephen, IV, 65

Martyrdom, in *Of Reformation*, X, 188–89
Martz, Louis L., *I, 115–34*
  on Donne, XI; 14
  on *PL*, V, 31, 208–09
  on *PR*, I, 52, 61; II, 86; IV, 177
  on *SA*, V, 150
Marullo
  —*Hymni Naturales*, VII, 179, 180
Marvell, Andrew, II, 79; XI, 17; XII, 188
  on *PL*, I, 93–94, 186
  on pleasure, VI, 53–54
  —*A Dialogue Between the Resolved Soul, and Created Pleasure*, VI, 53–54
  —"The Garden," X, 97
  —*Horatian Ode*, III, 4
  —"The Mower against Gardens," VIII, 30
  —"On Paradise Lost," XI, 9
  —*The Rehearsal Transpos'd*, VIII, 107, 115
Mary, IV, 14
  and Eve, VII, 268–69, 292–304, 305–06; XII, 19
  purification of, VIII, 152–53
  representations of, VI, 120–21
Mason, John B., *X, 23–33*
A Masque at Ludlow. See *Comus*
Masques
  artifice in, VI, 144–45
  Jonson's, VI, 144, 146
  parody in, VII, 32
  production of, V, 290–91
  purpose of, III, 201
Mass, Milton on, I, 141
Masson, David, V, 252; XII, 204, 206, 207
  on *Comus*, III, 206
  on Milton's career as public servant, XII, 167, 187
  on *Ad Patrem*, X, 40

Mather, Samuel, IV, 144–45; VII, 222, 228
"Matron," in *PL*, VI, 20n9
Matthew, St., Gospel of, II, 10; V, 69
  divorce in, VI, 199–200, 209, 210
  Nativity in, XII, 217, 218–20
  as source for *De Doctrina Christiana*, VIII, 191
  as source for *Lycidas*, IX, 234
  as source for *PL*, III, 180; VIII, 169–70
  as source for *PR*, VI, 237, 238, 239; VII, 196, 201; IX, 268
  as source for *SA*, V, 81–82
  as source for *Sonnet 18*, X, 175
Matthiessen, F. O., on Hawthorne, VI, 109
Mayer, Hans, VIII, 216, 217, 218
"Mazie error," I, 14n13
Meadows, Philip, XII, 184, 187, 188
Mede, Joseph, VI, 124, 132; XI, 74, 75
  —*Diatribae*, VII, 256–57
Medicine, seventeenth-century, II, 217. *See also* Imagery, medical
Melancholy
  in *L'Allegro* and *Il Penseroso*, III, 58; VII, 88–89, 90
  in landscape, VIII, 6.
  See also Mirth and Melancholy
Mellor, Anne Kostelanetz, on Blake, VIII, 145n2
Menander
  —*Peri Epideiktikon*, V, 47
Mercy, in *PL*, III, 162, 163–66; IV, 25; VIII, 273–79
Mery, Huon de
  —*Le Tornoiement de l'Antichrist*, VI, 133
Messenger (*SA*), I, 131–32; VII, 65–66, 73–74
Messiah, as military figure, XII, 246–47, 257–58

Metaphor
  in *Areopagitica*, II, 115–16; IX,
    190–93, 194
  in *Lycidas*, III, 21–22
  organic, I, 22, 24–26 (*see also*
    Organicism)
  in *PL*, I, 22–26; II, 180–81; III,
    152–55
  and ritual, I, 52–53
  St. Augustine on, X, 103–04
  spatial, I, 61–62
  spiritual, IV, 47–50.
  See also Imagery
Methodologies
  abuse of, VII, 12–14
  anachronism in, VII, 13
  innovation in, VII, 22–23
  interdependence of, VII, 22–24,
    29–30
  limits of, VII, 6, 8–9
  in Milton studies, VII, 3–27
  neglect of, VII, 12
  overreliance on, VII, 12–13
  as rhetoric, VII, 9–10
  in seventeenth century, VII, 4
  validity of, VII, 11–12.
  See also Criticism
"Methought I saw my late espoused
  Saint." See *Sonnet 23*
Meun, Jean de
  —*Roman de la Rose*, VII, 293,
    295; XII, 223
Michael, St., the Archangel, I, 143–
  44, 148; II, 53, 54
  and Adam, I, 45
  in *Comus*, VI, 133
  in *Lycidas*, III, 18
  and Moses, II, 13–14
  in *PL*, II, 13–14, 211–15; III, 56,
    126–27, 129, 139–41, 147–48;
    IV, 16–17, 209–10; V, 195, 198,
    210; VII, 220–21
  in Rightwise, VI, 125
  sonnets of, V, 133–34, 138–41

  on war, III, 171–72
Michaelmas, VI, 133, 135–36
Michelangelo, VIII, 30
  —*The Last Judgment*, I, 26–27
Midnight, in *PL*, VI, 267–68
Midrasch Rabba, IV, 209; VII, 256
Miller, David, on *L'Allegro* and *Il
  Penseroso*, IX, 217
Miller, Mark Crispin, X, 65–76
Miller, Milton, on *PL*, I, 28
Milton, John
  acquainted with Dryden, XI, 6–10
  anonymous biographer of, IX,
    250–51, 253
  apotheosis of, XI, 66–68
  audience of, I, 168–69, 174, 182–
    87; II, 60, 214, 216; IX, 3–36
  books read by, I, 33; IV, 119–21,
    125–26; VII, 21
  as Christian poet, II, 105
  at Christ's College, VII, 135–38
  death of, XI, 122
  and Diodati, VII, 127–63
  dissatisfied with church, VIII, 47,
    48–51
  education of, II, 116; X, 178
  effeminacy of, VII, 134–35, 136–39
  gardens of, V, 252, 259–60
  at Hammersmith and Horton, VII,
    145–47; VIII, 42–43, 44, 46–47,
    50–51, 53, 57; X, 151
  Hayman portrait of, VIII, 145–
    46n14
  homosexuality of, VII, 152–54
  identity crisis of, VII, 145–47,
    149–51
  influence of, XI, vii–xiv
  knowledge of Virgil of, I, 33
  letters of, II, 133–35; VII, 134,
    145–46, 155–57; VIII, 50, 58
  Marshall portrait of, X, 48–49
  as narrator of *PL*, XII, 86–87
  research on, VII, 4–5
  Romantic view of, XI, x–xiii, 45,

70–71, 77, 108
as secretary for foreign languages, XII, 165–95
self-image of, VII, 146–47
sexual experience of, VII, 133
studiousness of, VII, 134–35, 139
teaching of, VIII, 54–55, 64
travels to Italy, VIII, 53–54, 62–65; XII, 204, 205, 206, 207, 208
as type of Christ, XI, 63–65, 68–69
unidentified verse of, XII, 201–08
unity in poetry and prose of, I, 21
vocational choice of, III, 11–12, 21–24; V, 115; VII, 150; VIII, 41–69
Milton Studies, history of, XII, vii–xi
Mind
  in *Areopagitica,* V, 231
  development of, in *PL,* V, 229–48
  in Gnostic literature, XII, 16
  in Neoplatonism, XII, 17
  in Platonism, V, 232
Miner, Earl, *XI, 3–27*
Mirroring
  in Gnostic literature, XII, 16
  in *PL,* III, 109–11
Mirrors, and self-knowledge, III, 112–16
Mirth and Melancholy
  in *L'Allegro* and *Il Penseroso,* III, 58; VII, 78, 81, 95; IX, 209–18
  as subjects of illustration, VIII, 125, 127, 128–34, 136
Mitchell, Charles, on Dalila, X, 26
Mohl, Ruth, VI, 299
Mollenkott, Virginia R., *VI, 101–11*
  on Dalila, X, 29–30
Moloch, VIII, 178, 182
Moly, IV, 156–57; VI, 22, 24, 27; VII, 139; IX, 56–57
Monck, General, V, 271, 272
Monism, I, 135–36, 154–56
Montemayor, Jorge de
  —*Diana Innamorada,* VIII, 88

Monuments
  in *PL,* XII, 109
  in *SA,* XII, 107–09.
  See also Fame; Immortality
Moon
  after the Fall of Man, IX, 165
  allegorical interpretation of, IX, 155–56, 159
  in Blake's illustrations for *L'Allegro* and *Il Penseroso,* VIII, 134
  and blindness, IX, 164
  and Christ, IX, 158–64
  classical descriptions of, IX, 153
  in myth, IX, 154
  in Neoplatonism, IX, 159
  in *PL,* VI, 266–67; IX, 151–67
  in *Il Penseroso,* IX, 154; XII, 230
  Renaissance descriptions of, IX, 153–54
  and Satan, IX, 158–59
  scientific speculation on, IX, 155, 157
  symbolism of, IX, 39
  typology of, IX, 159, 163
Morality plays, I, 78; VI, 117. *See also* Mystery plays
More, Alexander, VIII, 91–92
  —*Fides Publica,* VIII, 94–96
More, Henry, X, 17; XI, 73–74
  —*Psychozoia,* III, 112–13
More, St. Thomas, VI, 48–49
On the Morning of Christ's Nativity. *See* Nativity ode
Mortalist heresy, VIII, 167, 173–74, 193, 196
"Mortal sting," I, 11
Mosaic law, in *SA,* III, 187–98; XII, 154–55
Moses
  in Acts of the Apostles, VII, 224–25
  in *Animadversions,* VII, 213
  in Apocrypha, VII, 214
  in *An Apology,* VII, 226
  in *Areopagitica,* VII, 211–12, 219

Moses *(cont.)*
    in *Biblia Pauperum,* VII, 273
    Calvin on, VII, 229
    in Christian tradition, VII, 209–10
    in Deuteronomy, VII, 225
    in *De Doctrina Christiana,* VII,
        210–11, 215–16, 225–26; IX,
        234–35
    in *Doctrine and Discipline of
        Divorce,* VII, 219, 226; VIII,
        84; IX, 234
    eloquence of, VIII, 250–51
    in Exodus, VII, 208, 210
    Ezekiel on, VII, 216
    in Hellenistic tradition, VII, 208–
        09
    Josephus on, VII, 209, 212, 214–15
    in *Lycidas,* IX, 225–34, 237
    Milton's identification with, III, 32
    in *PL,* I, 148; II, 12–16, 71–72;
        III, 164, 166, 167, 168; VII,
        207–32; X, 59
    Philo on, VII, 208–09, 211–12, 214
    Platonic view of, VII, 211–21
    and Raphael, II, 12–13
    in *The Reason of Church-
        Government,* VII, 215; VIII, 80
    St. Augustine on, VII, 210, 224
    and St. Michael, II, 13–14
    St. Paul on, VII, 222
    and Samson, II, 7
    seventeenth-century views of, VII,
        223
    Sidney on, VII, 212
    and Spirit, I, 148
    in Tasso, II, 87
    as type of Christ, II, 12–14; V, 69,
        75; VII, 209, 224–27; IX, 226
Mueller, Martin
    on *SA,* II, 216; XII, 121, 160
    on *Sonnet 23,* VIII, 151; X, 127
Mulciber, I, 37; IX, 82–83
Muldrow, George M., on *SA,* XII,
    160

Multiple choice, as Miltonic tech-
    nique, VI, 101–11. *See also*
    Ambiguity
Münster, Sebastian
    —*Cosmographiae Universalis,* X,
        82
Murdock, G. P., IV, 6, 10
Muse
    of Ariosto, III, 27
    failure of, XI, x–xi
    of history, X, 40–42
    of Homer, III, 27
    of *PL,* I, 147–50, 182–85; II, 62–
        63, 74–75; III, 26–32; IV, 202;
        V, 33
    Sicilian, III, 15, 50; IV, 153; IX,
        238–39
    Spenser's, III, 28
    Tasso's, III, 27–28
Muses, classical
    in *Arcades,* X, 38
    in *Lycidas,* II, 121–22; X, 38–39
    in *PL,* X, 39, 48, 53–55, 57–61
    in *Ad Patrem,* IX, 28; X, 36, 37,
        39, 40, 43–44
    in *Prolusion 7,* VI, 40–41
    in *The Reason of Church-
        Government,* V, 115
    tradition of, X, 35–38, 41–43, 48–
        53, 56–57
Music, IX, 42
    in *L'Allegro,* VII, 86–87; IX, 217
    in *Arcades,* VI, 45
    in *Comus,* V, 294, 307; IX, 65–66
    in Donne, IV, 169, 170
    in Dryden, XI, 16
    in *Lycidas,* IV, 159–60
    in Nativity ode, II, 107, 108, 110;
        IV, 169–70; VI, 51
    in *Ad Patrem,* IX, 217
    in *Il Penseroso,* VI, 45
Musica mundana, IV, 169–70
Mylius
    —*Tagebuch,* XII, 167, 178

Mystery, I, 168–69, 173–75
Mystery plays, VI, 113–14; X, 8
  as source for *Comus*, VI, 114–42
Myth, IX, 13–14
  defined, II, 24n1
  deformity in, IX, 69
  inversion of, in Milton, VI, 110
  Milton's use of, IV, 5–6; VI, 107,
    108
  and multiple choice, VI, 107–09
  in *PR*, VI, 223
  and ritual, I, 52–53
  of world parents, XII, 4–5
Myth-making, Milton's, VI, 109–10
Mythos, in epic theory, I, 70

Names
  in *PL*, I, 35, 182
  in *SA*, XII, 97
Narcissus, IV, 12; VII, 295–96, 299;
    XII, 12–13
  in *Comus*, VI, 172
  in Ovid, VI, 172
  in *PL*, IX, 90–93
  and self-knowledge, III, 108, 112,
    113, 114, 116–17.
  See also Eve, narcissism of
Napoleon, XI, x, 86, 87–89, 91–93, 95
Narration
  in *PL*, I, 107–10; II, 61; V, 29–33,
    43; VI, 283–90; VII, 207, 211,
    213, 216, 218, 226–28; IX, 98–
    100; XII, 86–87
  in *PR*, II, 83–101; VI, 228
Nationalism
  in *Areopagitica*, IX, 189
  in Milton and Isocrates, IV, 106–07
Nativity, XII, 217, 218–20. *See also*
  Nativity ode
Nativity ode, VII, 145
  and *Animadversions*, V, 106
  apocalypse in, IV, 170–71
  and *An Apology*, V, 110, 111
  astrology in, XII, 214, 223

battle in, IV, 170–71
biblical sources of, IV, 171–72
catalogue in, IV, 171, 174
chariot in, IV, 168
Christ in, IV, 165–66, 168, 171,
    173, 174; V, 77
Christian and pagan symbolism in,
    IV, 163–76
color in, III, 57, 61–62, 70, 76
dissonance in, IV, 170–71
dove in, IV, 165–68
dragon in, IV, 171
and *Elegy 6*, VII, 173
genre of, VII, 165–88
Hercules in, IV, 174
imagery of, II, 105–06, 108–10;
    V, 92–93, 122; VIII, 77
Incarnation in, IV, 163–64
introduction of, VII, 177
and Keats's *Ode to Psyche*, I, 103
landscape in, VIII, 12
Last Judgment in, II, 104, 109
light in, II, 105–06, 108, 110; IV,
    164–65, 168
as liturgical hymn, VII, 173–75,
    176–77
and Milton's poetic vocation, VIII,
    43
mood of, II, 103–04
music in, II, 107, 108, 110; IV,
    169–70; VI, 51
narrative in, VII, 177–79
nature in, IV, 165; IX, 44; X, 67
noise in, IV, 170–71, 172
as ode, VII, 166–67
pagan gods in, II, 8–9, 103–12;
    IV, 165, 168–69, 171–74; VI,
    107; VII, 179–81; IX, 44, 158
parody in, IV, 172–73
pastoral in, V, 119
peace in, IV, 165–67
poet in, IV, 171–72
and Pope's *Dunciad*, XI, 45
puns in, IV, 169

Nativity ode *(cont.)*
  and *The Reason of Church-
    Government*, V, 115, 116
  and *Of Reformation*, V, 104
  regeneracy in, V, 107, 112
  stars in, IV, 169
  structure of, IV, 171; V, 146
  sun in, IX, 44–46; XII, 230
  time in, II, 110–11; IV, 166
  typology in, IV, 170
  unity of, II, 106–08
  verse forms of, VII, 177
  water in, VIII, 20
  worship in, I, 170, 180
Nature
  in *L'Allegro* and *Il Penseroso*, IX,
    212
  and art, V, 259
  in *Comus*, VI, 16–17, 143–46; VII,
    33
  in epithalamic tradition, V, 53–54
  and grace, V, 121
  and knowledge of God, III, 111–12
  in *Lycidas*, V, 101
  as mother, IV, 7
  in Nativity ode, IV, 165; IX, 44;
    X, 67
  in *PL*, V, 217, 224, 230, 238
  in *The Reason of Church-
    Government*, V, 101
  in Tasso, III, 83–99.
  See also Landscape; Pastoral
Naunton, Robert, IV, 131
Nebuchadnezzar, X, 80–81, 83–88
"Negative formula," II, 39
Nelson, James G., XI, 83
Nelson, Leonard, on Socratic dialogue, VI, 220
Nelson, Lowry, Jr., on *Lycidas*, III, 6
Neoplatonism, VII, 177
  Alcestis in, VIII, 156–57; X, 131–
    32
  in *Comus*, VI, 129
  in *Lycidas*, III, 38–39

  in Milton, VI, 51
  mind in, XII, 17
  moon in, IX, 159
  pagan gods in, VIII, 156–57
  in *PL*, I, 153–62; V, 179–83, 184;
    VI, 294
  in *Il Penseroso*, VII, 88
  in *Sonnet 23*, VI, 182–83, 187–94
  in Tasso, III, 88–89.
  See also Platonism
Neptune, in *Comus*, V, 292; VI, 147
Neumann, Erich, IX, 38–39, 40, 41,
  57, 60–61, 62–63; XII, 4, 5
Neuse, Richard, on *Comus*, IX, 65
Nevo, Ruth, on heroic poetry, IX,
  106–07
New Dispensation
  in *De Doctrina Christiana*, IV,
    143–44; VII, 223–24
  and invisible church, IV, 82–83
  in *PL*, VII, 223
  in *PR*, VI, 230, 231, 239
  purification under, VIII, 158–59
  in *Sonnet 23*, IV, 143, 144, 145–46
Newman, John Henry, VI, 86, 98n4
Newmeyer, Edna, *XI, 83–98*
New Model Army, IV, 50–52, 53,
  54–55; V, 271
Newton, Thomas
  on *PL*, II, 30–31; VI, 260
  on *PR*, XII, 213, 225
Nicholas of Cusa, IX, 38
Nicholas of Dacia, XII, 223–25
Nicolson, Marjorie, on *PL*, III, 159
Night, in *PR*, IV, 180–81. *See also*
  Evening
Night-sea journey, IX, 60–62
Nimrod, IV, 22–23; XI, 93–95
Noah, in *PL*, V, 140
Noise
  in Nativity ode, IV, 170–71, 172
  in *PL*, X, 158–59, 160–61
  in *SA*, XII, 100
Noon, in *PL*, VI, 267–68; IX, 80–81,

82–83, 84, 85
Norford, Don Parry, *IX, 37–75; XII, 3–24*
North, Sir Thomas
—*Plutarch*, IV, 94
Northampton, Earl of, IV, 64–65
Northrop, Douglas A., *XII, 75–90*
Novation
—*On the Jewish Meats*, VII, 256
Numbers, Book of, II, 226
Numerology, III, 97; IX, 54–55, 269–70

Obedience
in *PL*, V, 180, 181, 195, 199; VIII, 223–24, 238, 240
in *Sonnet 19*, VIII, 244
In Obitum Praesulis Eliensis, V, 102, 103, 107, 124; XII, 230
Observations upon the Articles of Peace, IV, 123–24
Occasio, XII, 202–04
Of Christian Doctrine. See *De Doctrina Christiana*
Of Education. See under *Education*
Of Prelatical Episcopacy, X, 186–87
Of Reformation. See under *Reformation*
Ogden, H. V. S., III, 135
Old Comedy, XII, 95–97, 100–03, 109, 111
Oldenberg safeguard, XII, 179
Old Law, XII, 144–46
ceremonies under, VIII, 153–56
in *De Doctrina Christiana*, IV, 143–44; VII, 223–24
in *PL*, VII, 223
purification under, VIII, 158
in *Sonnet 23*, IV, 143–46
and visible church, IV, 82–83
Onkelos, IV, 197, 198
Onomatopoeia, in *PL*, III, 148–50
On Shakespeare. See under *Shakespeare*

On the Death of a Fair Infant. See under *Death*
On the Morning of Christ's Nativity. See Nativity ode
On Time. See under *Time*
Oporinus, John, VI, 119
Organicism
among Anglicans, IV, 89–91
in *Areopagitica*, IV, 97
in Christian theology, I, 155–56
in *Comus*, IV, 83
in Creation myths, I, 151–53
defined, IV, 79
in *De Doctrina Christiana*, VI, 122
in the Hermetica, I, 158
in *PL*, I, 22, 24–26, 151, 152–53, 156–58, 158–61; II, 22
among Puritans, IV, 89
in *The Reason of Church-Government*, IV, 90–91
in *Of Reformation*, IV, 83–84, 85–86, 89, 93–94, 95
in Renaissance, IV, 79–81
and the state, IV, 91–96
Origen, XII, 30–31, 260
Originality, XI, 24–25
Original sin, VI, 277–78, 280; VII, 244–45. *See also* Fall; Fall of Man
Orpheus, IX, 41–42, 65; XII, 12–13
in *Ad Patrem*, IX, 217
in *L'Allegro* and *Il Penseroso*, VII, 86, 93; IX, 215
and *Comus*, IX, 43–44
dismemberment of, I, 184–85
Dryden's use of, XI, 15–16
in *Lycidas*, II, 53; III, 11, 38–39; V, 74, 77; IX, 42–43; XI, 15
and *Sonnet 23*, X, 129, 132, 133
Ortelius, Abraham, atlas of, X, 80
Osiris, IX, 57–58; XI, viii–ix
in Nativity ode, IV, 173–74
Otten, Charlotte F., *V, 249–67*
"Overdaled," XII, 204–05
"Overdated," XII, 204–05

Overton, Richard, VIII, 120n16
  eschatology of, VIII, 198–99
  —*Araignment of Mr. Persecution,*
    VIII, 107
  —*Mans Mortallitie,* VIII, 198–99
Ovid, VI, 172; IX, 90
  on Circe, VI, 24–25, 25–26, 36–37
  as influence on *Elegy 1,* VI, 38–39
  Narcissus in, VI, 172
  —*Metamorphoses,* II, 32–33, 40;
    V, 41; VI, 36–37, 172
Ovington, John
  —*Voyage to Suratt,* VII, 251
Owen, John, VII, 245

Pacificism, in *Eikonoklastes,* VIII, 88
Pagan gods
  in Barlaeus, V, 57–58
  in Nativity ode, II, 8–9, 103–12;
    IV, 165, 168–69, 171–74; VI,
    107; VII, 179–81; IX, 44, 158
  Neoplatonists on, VIII, 156–57
  in *PL,* II, 48
  in Renaissance, VII, 180–81
Palmer, Thomas, IV, 54
Pan, in Nativity ode, IV, 169–70, 174
Pandemonium, I, 14n16; II, 79; VI,
  108–09; VIII, 30, 35
Panofsky, Erwin, on Virgil, VI, 261–62
Paradise
  air in, II, 41; V, 157–58, 251–52,
    255–57
  art in, VIII, 29–32
  bower in, V, 54–55, 156–57, 261–
    62; VII, 282–83; VIII, 21, 23–
    25, 29–30
  complexity of, VI, 299–300
  critical views of, VI, 299
  in Dante, II, 38–39, 49
  and death, V, 197
  destruction of, II, 52–53
  dynamism of, II, 42
  Eastern Gate of, VIII, 7–8; X, 78,
    84–87

  as English garden, V, 249–67;
    VIII, 4–25
  furnishings in, V, 260
  and Hanging Garden of Babylon,
    X, 81–84
  and heaven, V, 196
  and hell, VIII, 33–36
  hills in, II, 50, 75–78; V, 254–55;
    VIII, 5–7, 21–22; X, 78, 80–84
  as ideal, IV, 24
  irrecoverability of, V, 209
  location of, V, 254–55; VII, 270;
    X, 77–91
  Mount of, V, 254–55; VIII, 21–22;
    X, 78, 80–84
  orderliness of, II, 43–44
  and "paradise within," V, 205–08
  passions in, III, 130–32
  paths in, V, 260–61
  river in, II, 49; X, 78–80
  sexual intercourse in, V, 52–53,
    223; VI, 277–84
  in Sidney, II, 42–43, 44
  in Spenser, II, 39, 41, 42, 43, 44
  traditional depiction of, II, 38–39
  trees in, V, 255, 256–58, 263–64
  walls in, VIII, 6–8, 9
  water in, VIII, 17–20, 22–23, 36–
    37; X, 58–59, 78–80
  as womb, II, 22
  work in, V, 158–60, 262–64; VI,
    6, 7–8; VII, 285–86; IX, 111–12
Paradise Lost
  and Abraham, III, 164, 165, 167
  accommodation in, I, 23–24, 151,
    155; III, 160; VI, 93–97; VIII,
    210, 212, 271; X, 103
  action and contemplation in, I, 36,
    44
  "adhere" in, VII, 275–76
  allegory in, V, 79–80
  ambiguity in, II, 27; VIII, 166–76,
    181; XII, 20
  ambivalence in, I, 47–48

analogy in, II, 61
animals in, VIII, 26
animism in, VII, 250–51
anticipation in, I, 11–12
antifeminism in, IV, 14–15
apocalypse in, VIII, 172–76
"apparent" in, IX, 161
"arbiter" in, VI, 270–71
arguments to, VIII, 276–77; XI,
    5–7
Ariel in, IV, 210–13
Arminianism in, XII, 63–70
astrology in, XII, 214–15
audience of, I, 168–69, 174, 182–
    87; II, 60, 214, 216; IX, 3–36
authority in, IV, 8, 13, 14–16, 17,
    20–25
Azazel in, IV, 213–14
balance in, VI, 270
battles in, V, 28 (*see also* War in
    Heaven)
biblical sources of, I, 149, 150,
    152–53; II, 10–12, 180; III, 159–
    84; IV, 205–14; V, 21, 167, 198;
    VI, 108, 110; VII, 101–25, 211,
    213–14, 216–18, 222, 229, 233–
    34, 240–42, 258; VIII, 169–70,
    171, 188–90; IX, 52–55, 92; X,
    57; XII, 29–30, 35, 41
blindness in, II, 214–15; V, 32;
    X, 107
Book of Nature in, IV, 32–33;
    V, 183; X, 93, 95
Book III of, II, 176
Books XI and XII of, III, 139–58
brotherhood in, IV, 6–7, 22
and Byron's *Cain*, XI, xii
Calvinism in, XII, 48, 49–50
canzoni in, V, 138–39
catalogue convention in, I, 34–37;
    IX, 113, 114
catharsis in, II, 214–16
Catullus's influence in, V, 42–47,
    52, 53, 54, 57

Ceres in, V, 161–62
chariots in, III, 66–67, 76, 173–77,
    178; IX, 52–58, 66–67; XII, 230
chastity in, IV, 9
Circe in, VI, 54–65
color in, III, 56–57, 58, 59, 60, 61,
    62, 65–66, 66–67, 68, 69, 70,
    74, 154–55
comedy in, I, 22–23, 24–26, 104,
    106, 113; V, 18, 24, 27, 44–45;
    VIII, 215, 230–35; X, 5, 68,
    69–70
composition of, VIII, 266n25
conflicting ideas in, VI, 94
contemplation in, I, 36
contraries in, VII, 37–42
conversation in, VIII, 258–61
Copernican Revolution in, VI, 95–
    96
Creation in, IV, 32–36; VII, 270–
    77; VIII, 209–19
criticism of, I, 1–3, 15–16, 22; IX,
    77–103 (*see also* Criticism;
    Methodologies)
Cupid in, V, 56–57
death in, II, 33; VII, 242
deception in, I, 8
digression in, VI, 285–86
discipline in, IV, 54
as domestic epic, IX, 105–20
as drama, V, 3–37
dreams in, V, 233, 234–36, 237;
    X, 82–83; XII, 25–45
Dryden on, XI, 8, 17–19, 24
and Dryden's works, XI, 10–14
editions of, I, 7; XI, 9
education in, III, 140–41, 155–56;
    IV, 13–14; VI, 7; IX, 208; X,
    95–100, 102–03
and Eliot's works, XI, 119–21,
    127–28
and epic tradition, I, 3–4, 31–50;
    II, 212; V, 50–59
epistemology in, X, 93–109

Paradise Lost (cont.)
  epithalamia in, V, 39–66
  eternal torment in, VIII, 166–207
  eternity in, XII, 76, 85–86, 87–88
  ethos in, I, 76
  evening in, VI, 259–76
  Everyman in, V, 11, 15; VIII,
    217–18, 219
  evil in, I, 48, 93–94, 96, 108,
    112–13; III, 119–37
  faith in, VII, 238–39; IX, 122–23,
    127, 134, 146
  "fall" in, VIII, 221–46
  Fall of Man in, V, 19, 193–94,
    213–28; VI, 298; IX, 14–15; X,
    101–02
  fallen angels in, I, 85–88, 109–10;
    II, 77–78; VI, 107, 108–09; VII,
    252–53, 296; VIII, 284–85; IX,
    82–83 (*see also* Beelzebub;
    Belial; Satan)
  fire in, III, 56–57
  flowers in, I, 160; II, 40–41; III,
    75–76, 154; V, 156–62, 258–60;
    VII, 283; VIII, 11–12, 14–15
  food in, I, 135–37, 139–40; II, 13;
    V, 167–68, 184, 187
  forgiveness in, X, 161–62
  free will in, III, 104, 119–37; V,
    18, 19; IX, 137–39; XII, 49
  fruit in, III, 60, 152; IV, 155–56;
    V, 159–60, 165–71, 257, 258
  garden imagery in, V, 155–76; VII,
    270–72, 275, 277–78, 283, 286–
    87, 297, 306
  giants in, VIII, 183–84, 185–86,
    189
  gluttony in, IV, 185
  God in, III, 159–84; IV, 19–20,
    23–24, 25–32, 33, 36–37, 69–
    70; VII, 240; VIII, 271–72
  God's Word in, X, 157–58, 160
  grace in, XII, 49, 64–69
  "grateful" in, VI, 275n43

  and gunpowder conspiracy, IV,
    67–77
  harvest in, V, 171–72
  hell in, II, 51–52; III, 75; V, 12;
    VIII, 33–36, 174–76
  Hercules in, II, 32–33
  heroism in, I, 9–10, 41–44; IV, 20;
    V, 131–32; VIII, 183–86, 189;
    IX, 109–10, 115–18; XII, 48–49,
    68–69, 84
  Hesperus in, V, 24–43; VI, 264–
    65, 270–71; IX, 152, 153
  hierarchy in, IV, 21, 22; V, 166–
    67, 179–82, 187; VI, 6, 8; IX,
    15–24, 123–27; X, 96; XII, 3
  history in, I, 62; V, 182–83, 185–
    87, 191–92; XII, 87–88
  history play in, V, 23–29
  hospitality in, I, 135–37, 139–40,
    141–42
  humility in, VII, 268–69; X, 74–75
  and iconography, VII, 267–311
  identity of Creator in, VI, 103
  idleness in, VII, 295
  "image" in, VIII, 225–27; IX, 124
  imagery of, IX, 78, 80, 81, 82, 84
  imagery and metaphor in, V, 172–
    74
  imagination in, V, 233–47
  Incarnation in, IX, 96–97
  innocence in, III, 116, 119–37
  insects in, V, 165
  invocations of, I, 147–48, 149–50,
    152–53, 156–57, 182–85; II, 49,
    62–64, 75; III, 24, 25, 26–32;
    V, 30–33; VI, 94, 105; VII, 209,
    214, 216–18, 226–27; VIII, 20;
    XII, 79–82, 85, 86–87, 88–89
  irony in, IV, 69–72, 73–75; V, 9,
    32, 59–60, 246; VI, 105; VII,
    286; VIII, 240; XII, 40
  jealousy in, V, 219
  Judge in, VI, 103–04
  justice in, III, 162, 163–66; IV,

24–25, 29; VIII, 271, 272, 273–79
and Keats's works, XI, xii–xiii, 101, 104–05
kinship in, IV, 6–11, 13, 17–18; IX, 15–24
knowledge in, II, 30–31, 119–37; III, 127–28
knowledge of evil in, III, 119–37
landscape in, II, 37–58; V, 249–67; VIII, 3–40
language in, II, 89–90; IV, 8, 25–29; V, 172–74; VI, 300–01; VIII, 221–22, 247–66, 253–54, 256–57; IX, 129–30, 132; X, 104–06
Last Judgment in, II, 23; VIII, 167–76
law in, XII, 144–45
leadership in, VI, 13–14
liberty in, III, 197; VIII, 286–87; XII, 6–7
light in, II, 64–68, 80; III, 61, 68–69, 70, 72–77, 100, 168, 176–77; V, 31–32; VI, 105; VII, 216–18; VIII, 5–6, 35, 37–38; IX, 82; XII, 187
as literary pseudomorph, VII, 16
love in, III, 65–66; IV, 29–32, 34–36; V, 21, 222–25; VI, 191–92, 266, 268–69; VIII, 23–25
marriage in, IV, 9–11, 14–17; VI, 61–64; VII, 273–78; VIII, 258; IX, 110–11, 114–15
"matron" in, VI, 20n9
meal with Raphael in, I, 135–45
mercy in, III, 162, 163–66; IV, 25; VIII, 273–79
metaphor in, I, 22–26; II, 180–81; III, 152–55
midnight in, VI, 267–68
and Milton's translation of Psalm ii, III, 170–71, 179; IV, 69–72
mind in, V, 229–48

mirroring in, III, 109–11
monuments in, XII, 109
moon in, VI, 266–67; IX, 151–67
moral choice in, VI, 11–14, 17, 56
Moses in, I, 148; II, 12–16, 71–72; III, 164, 166, 167, 168; VII, 207–32; X, 59
muse of, I, 147–50, 182–85; II, 62–63, 74–75; III, 26–32; IV, 202; V, 33
muses in, X, 39, 48, 53–55, 57–61
myth in, VI, 107, 108–09, 110; VII, 244–45, 249–50, 253, 255, 262; VIII, 215
myth of exodus in, II, 3–26
names in, I, 35, 182
narration of, I, 107–10; II, 61; V, 29–33, 43; VI, 283–90; VII, 207, 211, 213, 216, 218, 226–28; IX, 98–100; XII, 86–87
as narrative, IX, 86–88, 95–96, 100–01
nature in, V, 217, 224, 230, 238
Neoplatonism in, I, 153–62; V, 179–83, 184; VI, 294
Noah in, V, 140
noise in, X, 158–59, 160–61
noon in, VI, 267–68; IX, 80–81, 82–83, 84, 85
obedience in, V, 180, 181, 195, 199; VIII, 223–24, 238, 240
Old Law in, VII, 223
organicism in, I, 22, 24–26, 151, 152–53, 156–58, 158–61; II, 22
pagan gods in, II, 48
and *PR*, IV, 185–87
"paradise within" in, V, 191–211
paradox in, I, 10–11, 15
parody in, VII, 37–42; VIII, 281–82; XII, 38
pastoral in, V, 19–23; VIII, 18; IX, 114, 119
phallic symbolism in, IX, 66–67
physical and moral equivalencies

Paradise Lost (cont.)

in, II, 68–71

plots of, V, 6

poet in, II, 59–82; VIII, 261–64

and Pope's works, XI, 33–45

posture in, VIII, 221–46

prayer in, I, 179; V, 169–70, 237;
VII, 226–29; VIII, 252; IX,
141–43

preface to, I, 53–54, 121–22

pride in, VI, 68

puns in, I, 25, 140; II, 28; IV, 74;
V, 160, 162, 172, 183, 234; X,
104–05, 159

purpose of, I, 167–68, 170, 172,
174–75, 182; II, 62; VIII, 212–
14; X, 57

rabbinical sources for, IV, 195–
215; XII, 17

rain in, V, 163

rainbow in, III, 154

reason in, III, 197; V, 233, 234–
35, 236–37, 238, 239–46; VI,
96, 294–95; XI, 39

redemption in, VII, 306

Red Sea in, II, 15; IX, 233

regeneracy in, VII, 52–53; VIII,
273, 275; X, 106; XII, 25–26,
28–29, 35

rhetoric in, I, 69–88; X, 177

rhetorical figures in, III, 141–51;
IV, 27

rhythm in, VIII, 253–57

rivers in, II, 49

salvation in, I, 7–8

Samson in, VI, 245; IX, 50

and SA, II, 179–81

satire in, I, 55, 56–58, 60; XI, 46

seed in, III, 152–53; V, 171

self-esteem in, VIII, 235–38

self-knowledge in, III, 103–18

sexual intercourse in, V, 53, 223;
VI, 277–78, 279, 282–98

sexuality in, I, 162–64; VI, 6, 265

and Shelley's *Alastor,* XI, x

snakes in, II, 27–35

as Socratic dialogue, IX, 89–101

soliloquy in, I, 72, 73–74, 80–81,
97–107, 110–12; III, 104; V, 5,
11, 14, 213–14, 215–18, 219–22;
VII, 52–53; VIII, 259; IX, 145;
X, 70–75

Solomon in, II, 78–80

sonnets in, V, 129–47

Spirit in, I, 147–57; III, 29–31;
VII, 229–30; X, 54–55

"stand" in, VIII, 221–46

stars in, V, 266–67

Stoicism in, V, 17, 26–27

storms in, V, 162–64

structure of, V, 19, 132–36, 140, 143,
146–47, 202; VII, 31–32; VIII,
214–15; IX, 78, 83–86, 87–88,
121–49; X, 132–33; XII, 75–90

student response to, IV, 19, 20

style of, I, 1–14

subject of, II, 73

sublime in, VIII, 20; IX, 151–52

submission in, IV, 8, 14–16

suicide in, VIII, 182–83; IX, 22

sun in, V, 163; IX, 46, 52–56

syntax of, I, 6–9, 10; VII, 30–31

tableaux in, VIII, 8, 27, 29, 32

Tacitus' influence in, IV, 129,
136–37

temptation in, II, 16–17; V, 19–
20, 214–15; VI, 290–91; VII,
300; XII, 26

time in, II, 23; V, 28, 42–43, 157,
171, 207–08; VIII, 215–16; IX,
87–88; XII, 76–79, 81, 85–86, 87

tragedy in, II, 212–14; V, 5–17;
VIII, 215

tragicomedy in, V, 19–23

tree analogy in, V, 177–90

Tree of Knowledge in, III, 60,
124–28; VII, 237–39, 240–42,
248–49

Tree of Life in, VII, 248–49
trees in, II, 40, 41, 44–45; III, 99;
V, 224; VIII, 14–15, 35–36
truth in, X, 101
typology in, I, 12; II, 76; V, 17,
74–75, 186; VII, 209, 210, 221–
30, 268–69; IX, 143–44
Urania in, I, 182–85; II, 66; V, 30;
VIII, 158, 263; IX, 159; X, 53–
55, 57–61
Uriel in, II, 65–66, 67; IV, 208–09
vainglory in, IV, 185
veils in, IX, 152, 164
"vicissitude" in, VI, 272
Virgil's influence in, I, 31–43, 46–48
"wander" in, II, 10, 68–70; IX,
78–80
wind in, VIII, 169–70
wisdom in, IV, 202–03; X, 57
women in, IV, 3–18 (*see also* Eve)
"wonder" in, IX, 133
and Wordsworth's works, XI, 87–
94
as worship, I, 167–77
worship in, I, 149, 170, 175–76;
VII, 282, 283–85.
See also Abdiel; Adam; Adam and
Eve; Chaos; Council in Heaven;
Eve; "Hail wedded Love";
Michael, St.; Paradise; Raphael;
Satan; Sin and Death; Son;
War in Heaven
Paradise Now, V, 5
Paradise Regained
action and contemplation in, IX,
273
animals in, VIII, 26
astrology in, XII, 213–14, 231
avarice in, IV, 183, 186–88
biblical sources of, VI, 227–41;
VII, 195–96, 201, 257; IX, 268;
XII, 125, 239
Christ and Adam in, IX, 261–75
Circe in, VI, 65–68

color in, III, 61, 70
contemplation in, VIII, 29
councils in, XII, 253–54
criticism of, I, 52, 61
dove in, IV, 182
as drama, IX, 272–73
and Dryden's *Absalom and
Achitophel*, XI, 12
evening in, VI, 273
fall of Satan in, VII, 198–99
first coming of Christ in, V, 203
food in, VII, 257; XII, 261–62
form of, VI, 215–16
fraud in, IV, 181
free will in, VII, 202; IX, 263–64
gluttony in, IV, 180, 181, 183,
185, 186, 187, 189
God in, II, 89–90
Hercules in, XII, 242–45
heroism in, V, 131
historicity of, XII, 235–51
irony in, IV, 191; V, 78; VI, 235–36
knowledge in, VI, 220–21
lack of charity in, VI, 52
landscape in, I, 61
light in, II, 94, 95, 97
liturgical sources of, VII, 196
multiple choice in, VI, 105, 106
myth and allegory in, VI, 223
myth of exodus in, II, 7
narrator of, II, 83–101; VI, 228
and Nebuchadnezzar's dream, X,
83, 85
New Dispensation in, VI, 230,
231, 239
night scenes in, IV, 180–81
and *PL*, IV, 185–87
parody in, VII, 42–44
pastoral in, VIII, 26
political background of, XII, 237–
38, 241, 248–49
and Pope's *Dunciad*, XI, 43
portents in, IV, 182
predestination in, IX, 263–64, 268

Paradise Regained (cont.)
  pride in, VI, 68
  prologue to, II, 83–85
  purpose of, II, 86; X, 57
  repetition in, VII, 197–98
  rhetoric in, I, 90; X, 178
  ritual in, I, 51–65
  Rome in, VI, 66
  sacrifice in, VI, 223
  and *SA*, II, 179; XII, 93, 104–05
  Satan in, II, 87–88, 95–99; IV,
    180, 181–82, 183–84, 186, 187,
    188–89, 190, 191; XII, 253–66
  satire in, XI, 46
  scriptural revelation in, IX, 267–
    68, 272
  and Shelley's *Prometheus*
    Unbound, XI, xi
  Sociamism in, IX, 263
  as Socratic dialogue, VI, 215–26
  soliloquy in, VI, 233–35; VII, 197,
    200–01; IX, 266
  sonnets in, V, 130, 131, 147–48
  spatial metaphor in, I, 61–62
  Spirit in, II, 85, 95; VI, 228
  "stand" in, VI, 232
  Stoic allusions in, XII, 241–45
  storm in, VIII, 26–27
  structure of, IV, 177–93; IX, 269–
    70
  Tacitus' influence in, IV, 129
  temptations in, I, 62; II, 88, 95–
    99; IV, 178–93; VI, 65–68, 218–
    21, 228; VII, 43–44, 194–96,
    202; IX, 264–65, 268–70
  theme of, II, 84
  time in, I, 62–64; VII, 189–205
  title of, IX, 262
  as tragicomedy, V, 25
  transitional passages in, IV, 182–83
  Tree of Jesse in, V, 185–86
  Tree of Life in, VI, 238
  typology in, V, 78–79; VII, 199;
    IX, 261–75; XI, 12

  Urania in, X, 61
  vainglory in, IV, 181, 183–84,
    185–86, 189
  violence in, IV, 181, 182.
  See also Christ
"Paradise within," I, 48; II, 8, 19,
  21, 54; III, 129; V, 163, 166, 171,
  172, 191–211; XII, 21
Paradox, in *PL*, I, 10–11, 15
Pareus, David
  on the moon, IX, 155–56
  on St. John, II, 212–13, 214
Parker, Matthew, VI, 118, 131
Parker, Samuel, VIII, 107
Parker, William Riley, V, 4–5
  on *Comus*, VI, 166
  on *Epitaphium Damonis*, VII, 158
  on Milton's career as public serv-
    ant, XII, 165, 166, 180, 187, 190
  on Milton's tone, X, 143–44
  on *Ad Patrem*, VIII, 60–61; X, 40
  on *SA*, IV, 60; X, 26–27; XII, 118
  on *Sonnet 23*, IV, 141, 142; VI,
    181; VIII, 149–50, 152, 159
Parkinson, John
  —*Paradise in Sole Paradisus*
    Terrestris, V, 250–52, 259, 262
Parliament
  in *Areopagitica*, IX, 189–90
  Long, V, 108, 110–12, 117, 124,
    271, 272; VII, 50–52; XII, 186
  Milton's attitude toward, IV, 104;
    V, 270, 271–73, 275–78, 279;
    VIII, 79; X, 204–09
  Rump, V, 271; X, 210
Parody
  in *Animadversions*, II, 117–18
  in *An Apology*, II, 117–18
  in *Areopagitica*, II, 115; VII, 36–37
  in *Comus*, VII, 32–36
  in masques, VII, 32
  in Milton's poems, VII, 32–48
  in Nativity ode, IV, 172–73
  in *PL*, VII, 37–42; VIII, 281–82;

XII, 38
in *PR*, VII, 42–44
in *Of Reformation*, III, 113–14
in *SA*, VII, 44–46
Pascal, Blaise
—*Provincial Letters*, XII, 261
The Passion, V, 104; VII, 142, 145
Passions, in Paradise, III, 130–32
Pastoral
in *L'Allegro*, VII, 85
in antiprelatical tracts, V, 99–100, 109, 110, 120
in epithalamia, V, 44, 54
evil in, V, 22
Fulgentius on, III, 40, 42–43
as genre of young poets, III, 36–37
in *Lycidas*, III, 5, 9, 11–20, 22, 26, 36, 39–40, 41–45, 47–51; IV, 152–53; V, 77, 98, 120
in Milton's early poetry, V, 119–20
and *PL*, V, 19–23; VIII, 18; IX, 114, 119
in *PR*, VIII, 26
in *The Reason of Church-Government*, V, 21–22
in Renaissance, II, 46–47
style of, III, 45–47
subgenres of, III, 43–45
theory of, III, 40–41
in Virgil, II, 45–46; III, 14–15, 36–37, 38, 40, 42, 43, 47.
See also Landscape; Nature
Patch, Howard Rollins, II, 39
Patchen, Kenneth
—"What is the Beautiful?" II, 4–5
Pathetic fallacy, in *Lycidas*, III, 10
Paths, in Paradise, V, 260–61
Patience, VI, 89–90
in *SA*, II, 167–68, 190; VI, 71–72, 74–75
in *Sonnet 19*, X, 143, 144–45
Ad Patrem
and *An Apology*, V, 110; VII, 50–52, 60

autobiographical content of, VII, 151, 157–58
dating of, VIII, 60–62
education in, IX, 207
muses in, IX, 28; X, 36, 37, 39, 40, 43–44
music and verse in, IX, 217
Orpheus in, IX, 217
poetry and prayer in, I, 180–82; IX, 43
wisdom and strength in, VII, 51
Patrick, J. Max, IV, 97
on Milton's career as public servant, XII, 166, 167
Patrick, John M., on Circe, VI, 22
Patrides, C. A., X, *3–21*; VIII, 224
on *Doctrine and Discipline of Divorce*, VI, 200
on *PL*, VI, 193; XII, 49, 68
on War in Heaven, I, 23
Patterson, Annabel, *VIII, 71–101*
Paul, Robert, on Cromwell, IV, 55
Paul, St.
on Adam and Christ, IX, 262–63
affliction of, X, 145–49
in *Areopagitica*, IV, 111–12
on authority, IV, 23
on charity, VI, 204
on childbearing, IV, 144
conversion of, XI, 59
on faith, V, 71–72
on law, XII, 142–43
on marriage, VI, 281–82, 287
military imagery of, IV, 47
on Moses, VII, 222
and myth of exodus, II, 6–7
and organicism, IV, 81–82, 96
on resurrection, VIII, 204n22
in *Second Defence*, X, 145
and *Sonnet 19*, X, 144–49
as source for *Areopagitica*, IX, 198, 199
as source for *De Doctrina Christiana*, VII, 223–24; IX, 244

Paul, St. *(cont.)*
　　as source for *Lycidas*, IX, 222,
　　　　225–26, 233, 235–36, 238
　　as source for *PL*, III, 179; VII, 229;
　　　　VIII, 171; IX, 92
　　as source for *PR*, VI, 230, 231–34,
　　　　236, 237, 238; XII, 239
　　as source for *Sonnet 23*, V, 76;
　　　　VIII, 160; X, 124
　　on toleration, IV, 102
　　vision of, IX, 229
　　—Colossians, III, 179
　　—Corinthians, I, 149; IV, 81–82,
　　　　96; V, 76; VI, 204, 233, 237,
　　　　281–82, 287; VII, 222; VIII,
　　　　160; IX, 262–63; X, 124, 145–49
　　—Ephesians, IV, 49; VI, 186, 191,
　　　　193, 232; VII, 192; IX, 244; X,
　　　　144
　　—Galatians, VI, 233–34; X, 146
　　—Hebrews, II, 6–7, 226, 227; IV,
　　　　146; VI, 189, 232–33; VII, 222,
　　　　229; VIII, 171; IX, 222, 225–26,
　　　　233, 235–36, 238; XII, 239
　　—Philippians, VIII, 171
　　—Romans, I, 174; IV, 23; V, 71–
　　　　72; VI, 194, 229–30, 231–32,
　　　　236, 238; VII, 223–24; IX, 244,
　　　　263; X, 144; XII, 142–43
　　—Timothy, IV, 144; V, 105; VI,
　　　　208, 238, 285; IX, 92, 198
Pausanius, XII, 197, 201
Peacham, Henry, VIII, 5
　　—*Minerva Britanna*, III, 60; VII,
　　　　290
Pecheux, Mother M. Christopher,
　　　　IX, 221–41; XII, 197–211
Pelagianism, VIII, 155; XII, 47, 52,
　　　　58, 65
Il Penseroso
　　ambiguity in, VII, 88–89
　　astrology in, XII, 214
　　contemplation in, VIII, 28
　　Goddess Melancholy in, VII, 88–

89, 90
　　imagery of, VIII, 13
　　landscape in, VIII, 13
　　light in, III, 73; VII, 87–88, 92
　　Milton's vocational choice in, VIII,
　　　　55–56
　　moon in, IX, 154; XII, 230
　　music in, VI, 45
　　Neoplatonism in, VII, 88
　　perception in, VII, 92–93
　　Platonism in, V, 120
　　and Pope's *Epistle to Burlington*,
　　　　XI, 36
　　reading of, VII, 87–95
　　sound in, VIII, 13.
　　See also *L'Allegro* and *Il Penseroso*
Il Penseroso, identity of, VII, 95
Penz, Georg, VII, 299–300
Pequigney, Joseph, on *Sonnet 19*, X,
　　　　141
"Perfect Glorification," V, 201–05
Peri gamou, V, 49, 55–59
Perkins, William, IV, 43
　　on marriage, VI, 282
　　—*The Arte of Prophecying*, XI, 77
Perlette, John M., X, 195–215
Peter, John, V, 217
　　on *PL*, III, 159; IX, 94, 100; XII,
　　　　49, 63
Peter, St.
　　deliverance of, XI, 59–60
　　in *Lycidas*, II, 123–24, 125–26; III,
　　　　14–17, 20, 37, 42, 43, 44, 47,
　　　　48–50; IV, 152; V, 77; IX, 223–
　　　　24, 234–35, 237
　　on purification, VI, 186
　　as source for *PL*, VIII, 189
　　—Second Epistle General of, VIII,
　　　　189
Petrarch
　　—*Sonnet 276*, X, 138–39n22
Phaeton, III, 173, 174; IV, 168, 174
Phallic symbolism, IX, 56, 57–58
　　in *Eclogue 7*, VII, 154

in *Epitaphium Damonis*, VII, 130, 131, 132
in *Lycidas*, VII, 153
in *PL*, IX, 66–67
Pharaoh, III, 163, 173
as type of Satan, II, 11, 19, 71–72
Pharisaic heresy, XII, 262
Philippians, Epistle to, VIII, 171
Philistian Officer (*SA*), II, 166–67, 191
Phillips, Edward, II, 131; V, 5, 21; VII, 133, 163n43; VIII, 54, 64
Phillips, John, VII, 133, 163n43; VIII, 54, 64; XI, 122
Philo (Judaeus), I, 151, 158; IX, 38, 54
on Moses, VII, 208–09, 211–12, 214
Philomel(a)
in *L'Allegro* and *Il Penseroso*, V, 74
in *Comus*, VI, 171–72
Philo of Byblos, IX, 50
Philostratus
—*Life of Apollonius of Tyana*, IX, 48
Phineas, in *An Apology*, IV, 196–97
Phoebus
in *Lycidas*, III, 13, 48; IV, 151–52, 153, 155, 157–59; V, 77; IX, 237, 238–39
in Nativity ode, IV, 168, 174
Phoenix
in *Areopagitica*, IX, 198
in Ramsey, V, 49–50
in *SA*, II, 208; VI, 256; VII, 69, 71; IX, 51; X, 27
in Tasso, III, 96
Picard, Jeremie, IX, 250
Piccolomini, Alessandro, X, 187
Pico della Mirandola, Giovanni
on Alcestis, V, 180–81; VIII, 156–57; X, 132
—*Against the Astrologers*, XII, 223

—*Commento sopra una canzona de amore*, X, 132
Picturesque, in landscape, VIII, 4–19
Piedmont Massacre, X, 170–71; XII, 182. See also *Sonnet 18*
Pilgrimage motif, III, 83–99; IX, 78
in Blake's *Milton*, XI, 62–63, 68–69
Pindar, VII, 169, 170
Piper, O. A., III, 128
Pirkê de Rabbi Eliezer, VII, 250, 297
Plants, in *Lycidas*, III, 7–9, 13, 38, 39, 41, 44–45; IV, 153–54, 156–57. See also Flowers; Trees
Plato, IX, 37–38
on Alcestis, X, 130
on Creation, I, 153–54
on harmony, I, 188–89n14
on knowledge, VI, 220
myth of exodus in, II, 9
on rhetoric, X, 179–80
Socratic dialogue of, VI, 216–17
—*Apology*, VI, 219
—*Charmides*, VI, 217
—*Cratylus*, I, 74
—*Crito*, VI, 222
—*Epistle VII*, VI, 220
—*Euthyphro*, VI, 217
—*Meno*, VI, 221
—*Phaedo*, VI, 146, 162, 163, 223
—*Phaedrus*, VI, 220, 223; IX, 55; X, 179–80
—*Protagoras*, VI, 217
—*Republic*, II, 9; IV, 92; VI, 217–18, 223; X, 37
—*Symposium*, VI, 217
—*Theaetetus*, VI, 222–23
—*Timaeus*, I, 153–54
Platonism, III, 114; V, 69
in *Comus*, V, 120
light in, IX, 37–38
mind in, V, 232
Moses in, VII, 211–21
in *Il Penseroso*, V, 120.
See also Neoplatonism

Pleasure
  in Circean temptation, VI, 25
  Marvell on, VI, 53–54
Pliny, II, 31; VIII, 32; X, 79–80, 84
  —*Natural History*, III, 66
Ploce, in *PL*, III, 144–46
Plotinus, V, 178–79; IX, 38, 56; XII, 17
Plummer, John, VII, 272
Plutarch, IV, 174
  on muses, X, 59
  —*De Pythiae Oraculis*, X, 39
Pocock, J. G. A., on Anthony Ascham, X, 195–96
Poet
  in *L'Allegro* and *Il Penseroso*, IX, 106
  masculinity of, IV, 7
  as minister, VIII, 210
  in *PL*, II, 59–82; VIII, 261–64
  as prophet, IV, 171–72; X, 148
  in *SA*, III, 24
  and shepherd, X, 59
  in Tasso, III, 87
Poetry
  Arnold on, XI, 106–07
  as calling, III, 4, 7, 11–12, 19, 21–25, 32; V, 120–21
  classical, Renaissance reinterpretation of, VII, 15–16
  devotional, I, 172
  Milton on, I, 176–77; III, 4
  and ministerial career, VIII, 41–43, 45, 62, 66–67 (*see also* Milton, John, vocational choice of)
  in *The Reason of Church-Government*, III, 19; V, 209
  role of, III, 18–19
  and theology, I, 51–52
  and worship, I, 176–82
Poimandres, XII, 15–16
Pointon, Marcia, XI, 69–70
Polanus
  —*Syntagma*, IX, 255

Polemics, Milton's, V, 270–71
Polybius, II, 136–38; V, 26
Polydore Vergil, IV, 127, 128, 132, 133
Polyptoton, in *PL*, III, 142–44
Pontano, hymns of, VII, 173
Pope, Alexander, I, 13*n1*
  on blank verse, XI, 30–31
  on Milton's God, XI, 51
  on Milton's imitators, XI, 31–32
  Milton's influence on, XI, viii, 29–50
  on *PL*, XI, 29–30
  on *PR*, XI, 30
  translations of Homer by, XI, 30, 32, 33–35
  —*The Dunciad*, XI, viii, 41–45
  —*Eloise to Abelard*, XI, 33
  —*Epilogue to the Satires*, XI, 36
  —*Epistle to Bathurst*, XI, 36
  —*Epistle to Burlington*, XI, 36
  —*Epistle to Dr. Arbuthnot*, XI, 36
  —*The Essay on Man*, XI, xviii, 36–39
  —*Imitations of Horace*, XI, 31, 35
  —*Moral Essays*, XI, 35
  —*Pastorals*, XI, 32
  —*The Rape of the Lock*, XI, viii, 40–41
  —"Windsor Forest," II, 43, 44; XI, 40
Pope, Elizabeth, on *PR*, I, 52; IV, 177–78, 185; IX, 264
Pope, the, in gunpowder poems, IV, 67, 68–69; V, 92
Popper, Karl, VI, 88
Portents, in *PR*, IV, 182
Portugal committee, XII, 170, 175
Posidippus, XII, 201, 205
Posture
  in *PL*, VIII, 221–46
  in *SA*, IV, 41
Poussin, Nicolas, II, 47

Powell, Mary, IV, 141; VI, 186; VII, 133; VIII, 150

Pratt, Alice Edwards, III, 71

Prayer
in *Animadversions*, VIII, 111–12
in *De Doctrina Christiana*, VII, 227; X, 169
in *PL*, I, 179; V, 169–70, 237; VII, 226–29; VIII, 252; IX, 141–43. *See also* Biblical lament; Worship

Predestination, I, 63
Calvin on, XII, 53–55
in *PR*, IX, 263–64, 268

Of Prelatical Episcopacy, I, 18–19
authority in, X, 185, 186–87
corruption in, V, 102

Price, Alan F., on *Areopagitica*, IX, 169, 185

Price, Sir Uvedale, on landscape, VIII, 4, 5, 11, 12, 16, 17, 18

Pride
Adam's, V, 12–13
in *PL* and *PR*, VI, 68
in Pope, XI, 39
in *SA*, II, 161, 167; III, 193
Satan's, I, 8, 101, 107, 109; V, 13; VII, 268, 296; X, 156

Priesthood, in *Lycidas*, III, 42

Prince, F. T., on *SA*, XII, 91, 92

Privy Council, VI, 118

Proclus
—*Commentary on the Chaldean Oracle*, VII, 176

Prolusions, rhetoric in, X, 178–79

Prolusion 1, IV, 103, 104, 111–12; V, 88

Prolusion 3, I, 178; V, 88
education in, IX, 205–06
history in, II, 132

Prolusion 4, V, 88

Prolusion 6, V, 88
autobiographical content of, VII, 136, 137
imagery of, V, 91, 100, 122

Prolusion 7, IV, 103, 107, 108, 112; V, 88; VII, 145; IX, 46; XI, 125
and *An Apology*, V, 110
Circe in, VI, 40–41
education in, IX, 204, 206–07
muses in, VI, 40–41

Prometheus, XII, 12–13

Prophecy, in *Lycidas*, III, 43

Pro Se Defensio, VIII, 94–97

Proserpina, in *PL*, V, 161

Proverbs, as source for *PL*, IV, 202–03, 204; X, 57

Prudentius
—*Liber Cathemerinon*, VII, 174, 178
—*Peristephanon Liber*, VII, 173, 174

Prynne, William
—"A Christian Paradise," V, 261
—*The Chvrch of Englands Old Antithesis To New Arminianisme*, XII, 60
—*A Looking-Glasse for all Lordly Prelates*, IV, 86
—*Lord Bishops, None of the Lord Bishops*, IV, 95

Psalms
as source for *Lycidas*, IX, 226–27
as source for *PR*, VI, 234–35; XII, 125
as source for *The Reason of Church-Government*, XII, 125
as source for *SA*, XII, 128–29

Psalm ii
Milton's translation of, IV, 69–72
as source for *PL*, III, 170–71, 179

Psalm xvii, VI, 193

Psalm xlix, VI, 278

Psalm li, XII, 133

Psalm lxv, VI, 267

Psalm lxviii, III, 177

Psalm lxxii, IV, 167

Psalm lxxx, Milton's translation of, XII, 126–27

Psalm lxxxiv, Milton's translation of, II, 76
Psalm lxxxvi, Milton's translation of, XII, 127
Psalm lxxxviii, Milton's translation of, XII, 128
Psalm cxiv, II, 10
Milton's paraphrase of, IX, 232–33
Psalter, XII, 125
Pseudepigrapha, VII, 297; VIII, 184, 186–89
Pseudomorphs
defined, VII, 14
in literary criticism, VII, 14–16
PL as, VII, 16
Psychology, seventeenth-century, III, 7; V, 231, 232–33, 237; XII, 26–27, 28, 39
Ptolemaeus, Claudius
—Geographia, X, 79–80
Puns
in Colasterion, VIII, 117
in Comus, IX, 46
as corruption of language, VIII, 255
in Elegy 1, VII, 137–38
in Marprelate, VIII, 105
in Milton's letters to Diodati, VII, 155–57
in Nativity ode, IV, 169
in PL, I, 25, 140; II, 28; IV, 74; V, 160, 162, 172, 183, 234; X, 104–05, 159
in Prolusion 6, VII, 137
in Second Defence, VIII, 91
in Sonnet 4, VII, 144
in Sonnet 7, VIII, 45
Purchas, Samuel
—Purchas his Pilgrimage, VII, 251; VIII, 257
Purification
in Book of Leviticus, VI, 185–86; VIII, 152
Calvin on, VIII, 155

Christ and, II, 226
in De Doctrina Christiana, VIII, 154–55
of Mary, VIII, 152–53
in Revelation, VI, 186; VIII, 152
St. Peter on, VI, 186
in SA, II, 226–27
in Sonnet 23, IV, 143–45; V, 75; VI, 185–86; VIII, 149–63; X, 119, 134–35
Puritan revolution, IV, 39–62
Puritans
on church and state, IV, 92–96
Donne on, IV, 89, 90, 91
iconoclasm of, IV, 88–89
on idleness, IV, 43–44, 45–46
on organicism, IV, 89
theology of, IV, 41–46, 55
Puttenham, George
on biblical lament, XII, 130–31
—Arte of English Poesie, V, 47
Pyle, Fitzroy, IV, 143; X, 134
on Sonnet 23, VIII, 150, 152–53
Pyrrhonism, VI, 99n15

Quarles, Francis
—Emblemes, VII, 287–91, 297–98, 302, 305
Quintilian, IX, 171; X, 180, 181
Quintilianus, Aristides, IX, 42
In Quintum Novembris, IV, 63, 66–70, 72; V, 91–93, 122; XII, 261
Qvarnström, Gunnar, IX, 52–53

Rabanus Maurus, IX, 155, 159
"Rabbinic Bible," Samson in, III, 187–89
Racovian Catechism, VIII, 197–98, 200; XII, 263
Raimondi, Marcantonio, X, 48, 51; XII, 202
Rain, in PL, V, 163
Rainbow, in PL, III, 154
Rajan, B., I, 1–14; VII, 29–48; XI,

vii–xiv, 115–29
on *PL*, VIII, 269; IX, 88, 140
on *PR*, VI, 227
Ralbag. *See* Ben Gerson, Rabbi Levi
Raleigh, Sir Walter, on *PL*, XI, 108
Ramistic method, IX, 244, 246, 251
   defined, VI, 207
   Milton's use of, VI, 201, 206–08;
      X, 179–81, 187
Ramsey, Andrew
   —*Poemata Sacra*, V, 49–50, 54
Ramus, Peter, VI, 206. *See also*
   Ramistic method
Randolph, Thomas, V, 62
Ransom, John Crowe, on *Lycidas*,
   III, 41
Raphael
   on accommodation, I, 23–24
   account of Creation by, VII, 102–
      21
   on earth and heaven, III, 83–84, 99
   on good and evil, III, 123–24, 126–
      27
   as guest of Adam and Eve, I, 135–
      36, 139–40
   and Moses, II, 12–13
   in *PL*, II, 211–13, 215; III, 65,
      169; V, 194–95, 238–39; VI,
      286–87, 293–98; VII, 219–20
   and Satan, XII, 38–39
   sonnet of, V, 134–35
   tree analogy of, V, 178–88
Rashi (Rabbi Solomon ben Isaac),
   III, 187; IV, 198–99, 205–08, 209–
   10, 210–11, 211–12, 212–13
Rationalism
   and imagery, V, 68–69, 73–74
   Milton's, V, 70
Readie and Easie Way, X, 182, 186;
   XII, 147
   education in, V, 283
   history in, V, 279–80
   irony in, V, 284, 286
   and "Letter to a Friend," V, 277–78

liberty in, V, 282–83, 284–85
publication of, V, 271–72
structure of, V, 278–85
style of, V, 75–78, 279, 282, 283,
   284
Realism
   Aristotelian, V, 69
   in *Comus*, VI, 148
   in depictions of Paradise, II, 38
Reason
   in Ariosto, VI, 27–28
   and choice, III, 120; IV, 111
   and imagination, XII, 39
   in *PL*, III, 197; V, 233, 234–35,
      236–37, 238, 239–46; VI, 96,
      294–95; XI, 39
   in Pope's *Essay on Man*, XI, 39
   in *SA*, II, 162, 163, 164, 173n16;
      III, 190–93, 196, 197–98
   in Spenser, VI, 35
   symbolized by moly, VI, 22
   and tyranny, VI, 55
The Reason of Church-Government,
   I, 182–83
   and *Arcades*, V, 93–94
   authority in, I, 19
   autobiography in, V, 113–16; VIII,
      42
   ceremony in, VIII, 154
   church in, IV, 82–83, 92–93
   and *Comus*, V, 94, 97, 109
   controversy in, X, 182
   discipline in, IV, 54
   and *Elegy 1*, V, 115
   and *Elegy 4*, V, 109
   and *Elegy 6*, V, 115
   epic in, X, 44
   and *Epitaphium Damonis*, V, 109
   genres in, VII, 168–70
   heroism in, VIII, 80–82, 93
   history in, II, 132–33, 144
   imagery of, V, 109–10, 113
   imagination in, V, 233
   irony in, V, 87–88, 114–15

The Reason of Church-Government
(cont.)
  and *Lycidas*, V, 99, 101
  Milton's vocational choice in, VIII,
    52–53, 62–63, 66–67
  Moses in, VII, 215; VIII, 80
  muses in, V, 115
  and Nativity ode, V, 115, 116
  nature in, V, 101
  organicism in, IV, 90–91
  pastoral in, V, 21–22
  poetry in, III, 19; V, 209
  prose in, V, 87–88
  psalms in, XII, 125
  purgation in, II, 222
  regeneracy in, V, 109–10, 111
  Revelation in, VI, 114
  rhetoric in, I, 90
  Samson in, IX, 47
  self-esteem in, VIII, 243
  and *Sonnet 7*, V, 113
  structure of, X, 190
  syntax of, V, 273–75, 283, 285
  temperance in, II, 220
  truth in, III, 6–7
  worship in, I, 171–72
  writer as minister in, VIII, 210
  writing of, XII, 199
Réau, Louis, VII, 279
Rebellion
  Calvin on, IV, 23
  Milton on, II, 73
Recognition scenes, I, 42, 43
Redemption, VII, 306
Red Sea, II, 15; IX, 225, 226–28,
  230–33
Reesing, John, on *Lycidas*, IX, 222
Reeves, Marjorie, XI, 66
Reformation
  and divorce, X, 205–09
  Milton on, IV, 97.
  See also *Of Reformation*
Of Reformation, IV, 104; XII, 147
  and *Arcades*, V, 94, 104, 109

  authority in, I, 17–18; X, 185
  baptism in, XII, 255
  "bishop" in, X, 189–90
  ceremony in, VIII, 154
  and *Comus*, V, 95–97, 104, 109
  councils in, XII, 253
  and *Elegy 4*, V, 108
  and *Epitaphium Damonis*, V, 109
  heroism in, VIII, 77–78
  imagery of, V, 104–05; VIII, 76–77
  Last Judgment in, I, 27–28
  liberty in, V, 270
  and *Lycidas*, V, 98, 99, 100, 104–
    05, 109
  martyrdom in, X, 188–89
  and Nativity ode, V, 104
  organicism in, IV, 83–84, 85–86,
    89, 93–94, 95
  "overdated" in, XII, 204
  patristic authors in, XII, 220
  and *In Quintum Novembris*, V,
    91–92
  regeneracy in, V, 104–05, 108–09,
    111
  rhetoric in, X, 188–90
  and Spenser's *Faerie Queene*, VIII,
    76–77
  stylistic parody in, II, 113–14
  truth in, I, 17–18, 28; III, 6
  and *At a Vacation Exercise*, V, 92
  worship in, I, 171
Regeneracy
  in *L'Allegro* and *Il Penseroso*, V,
    103, 107, 112
  in antiprelatical tracts, V, 87–127
  in Arminianism, XII, 56–57
  and catharsis, II, 216, 219
  in *Comus*, V, 97, 107, 112, 120, 124
  in *De Doctrina Christiana*, II, 152,
    157, 160, 227–28; V, 203–04;
    VII, 54
  individual, V, 106–16, 124
  in Milton's poetry, V, 88, 102, 103,
    104, 107, 112, 124

national, V, 106, 107–08, 112–13, 124–25
  in *PL*, VII, 52–53; VIII, 273, 275; X, 106; XII, 25–26, 28–29, 35
  and reformation of church, XII, 35
  in *SA*, II, 149–74; III, 191; VII, 55; XII, 141, 142
Remonstrance of 1610, XII, 55–59
Renaker, David, *XII, 213–33*
Renato, Camillo, VIII, 193
Repetition, in *PR*, VII, 197–98
Repton, Humphry, on landscape, VIII, 4, 5, 6, 7, 8–9, 15, 16
Republicanism
  Christ's, XII, 245–46
  Satan's, II, 73
  in Tacitus, IV, 119
Respublica, XII, 203
Restoration, the, V, 271, 272, 276, 278, 280; VIII, 72; XII, 62
Resurrection, II, 5, 7, 19–21; VIII, 195–96, 204n22; XI, 74–75
Revard, Stella P., *IV, 63–77*
  on War in Heaven, IV, 49–50
Revelation, scriptural, in *PR*, IX, 267–68, 272
Revelation of St. John the Divine. *See* John the Divine, St., Revelation of
Reynolds, Edward, XII, 28
Rheims New Testament, VI, 120, 121
Rhetoric
  in *An Apology*, X, 183
  Aristophanes on, I, 68–69
  Aristotle on, X, 180, 181, 184, 187, 202, 203
  in *Comus*, VI, 16–17
  in *Doctrine and Discipline of Divorce*, X, 192, 201–02
  in *Of Education*, X, 177–78, 179–80
  and history, II, 133–35, 137, 138–39, 140, 141, 143–44
  Longinus on, X, 180
  military, I, 82

Milton on, I, 16, 20; X, 177–93
Milton's training in, X, 178
Milton's use of, I, 67–68, 88–91
modern attitudes on, I, 67–68
  in *PL*, I, 69–88; VI, 8; X, 177
  in *PR*, I, 90; X, 178
Plato on, X, 179–80
  in the prolusions, X, 178–79
  in *The Reason of Church-Government*, I, 90
  in *Of Reformation*, X, 188–90
Satan's, I, 69–88; VI, 14–15, 219, 220
  and truth, I, 69–88, 90
Rhyme, IX, 112
  in drama, I, 53
Dryden on, I, 53–54
Milton on, I, 53–54, 121–22, 133n6; XI, 5–6
  in *SA*, I, 120–22, 125, 129–30, 132, 133; XII, 94
Rhythm, in *PL*, VIII, 253–57
Ribner, Irving, on history play, V, 24, 25, 26
Rich, Barnaby, IV, 50
Richardson, Jonathan
  —*Explanatory Notes and Remarks on Paradise Lost*, XI, 8
Richardson, Lady, on Wordsworth, XI, 83, 84
Richardson, Samuel
  —*A Discourse of the Torments of Hell*, VIII, 198
Ricks, Christopher
  on *PL*, I, 2, 140; VI, 300; IX, 98
  on *SA*, V, 80–81
Riggs, Edith, on *L'Allegro*, VII, 80–81
Riggs, William G., *II, 59–82; IV, 151–61*
Rightwise, John, VI, 125–26
"Rigid," VII, 243
Rime royal, VII, 177
Ripa, Cesare
  on muses, X, 41–42

Ripa, Cesare *(cont.)*
—*Iconologie,* III, 58, 59, 61; X,
    41–42
Ritual, IV, 85
    and drama, I, 52, 62
    and metaphor, I, 52–53
    and myth, I, 52–53
    in *PR,* I, 51–65.
    See also Ceremony
Rivers, in Paradise, II, 49; X, 78–80
Robertus Stephanus, on muses, X, 41
Robespierre, XI, 89–91
Robotham, John, XII, 33
Rogers, Richard, II, 221; IV, 43, 44
Rohde, Eleanour, on English gardens,
    V, 251–52, 261
Rollin, Roger B., *V, 3–37*
Rollinson, Philip, *VII, 165–88*
Rollock, Robert
    —*A Treatise of Gods Effectual
    Calling,* VII, 235
Romances, chivalric
    and *L'Allegro* and *Il Penseroso,* IX,
        212–13
    heroism in, II, 157; IX, 106–09
    Milton on, VIII, 83–84, 88–89
Roman de la Rose, VII, 293, 295;
    XII, 223
Romans, Epistle to. *See* Paul, St.
Romantics, on Milton, XI, x–xiii, 45,
    70–71, 77, 83–85, 86, 88, 108.
    See also Blake, William
Rome, depravity of, in *PR,* VI, 66
Roscelli, W. J., VII, 172
Rose, Edward J., on Blake, VIII, 124,
    142–43, 146*nn17, 22, 23,* 147*n28*
Rose, symbolism of, VII, 293–94
Rosenberg, D. M., *II, 113–18*
Rosenblatt, Jason P., *VII, 207–32*
Rosenmeyer, Thomas, VII, 96–97
Ross, Alexander
    on *PR,* XII, 259–60
    —*Pansebeia,* XII, 259–60

Ross, Malcolm M., V, 68, 69; VII, 172
Royal Society of London for Improv-
    ing Natural Knowledge, V, 225
Ruar, Martin, VIII, 197
Rule of charity
    Calvin on, VI, 204
    in divorce tracts, VI, 199–214
    in Erasmus, VI, 200, 202–04
    in St. Augustine, VI, 201–02
    source of, VI, 200–01, 202, 203–04,
        205–06
Rule of justice, X, 207–08
Rump Parliament, V, 271; X, 210
Ryken, Leland, on *PL,* IV, 32; VI,
    103–04
Rymer, Thomas
    —*Tragedies of the Last Age,* XI,
        17, 18

Sabbatarianism, IV, 43–44
Sabbath, in *SA,* IV, 44
Sabrina, VI, 134–35
    in *Comus,* V, 290, 299, 303–05; VI,
        147, 160–62, 177; IX, 27, 65–66
Sackville, Thomas, First Earl of
    Dorset, XI, 8
Sackton, Alexander, on *PR,* IV, 189
Sacrifice
    in *PL,* VIII, 279
    in *PR,* VI, 223
    in *Sonnet 23,* VI, 184–87
Safer, Elaine B., *VI, 215–26*
Salkeld, John, VI, 281
    —*A Treatise of Paradise,* VII, 255
Sallust, Milton on, II, 132, 133–34,
    135; IV, 119–20, 124–25
Salmasius, IV, 125–26
    Milton's attack on, I, 20
Salvation, I, 185–86
    in *De Doctrina Christiana,* II, 226
    in *PL,* I, 7–8
    in *Sonnet 23,* VI, 181–97; VIII,
        153; X, 119

Samson
    and Adam, II, 219–20, 227, 228;
        VII, 59
    in *Areopagitica*, IV, 39–40; VI,
        246; IX, 49
    biblical account of, VI, 245, 246,
        247, 256
    blindness of, I, 117, 118–19, 124–
        25, 127; II, 222; V, 81; VI, 249
    and Chorus, I, 116–22, 125–26,
        129, 131–33; VII, 61–63; XII,
        141–63
    and Christ, II, 224, 227–28; XII,
        104–05
    and Dalila, I, 126–28; X, 24–26,
        28; XII, 98–99, 100
    despair of, II, 153, 156, 159, 161
    faith of, XII, 129–30
    in *First Defence*, IV, 40
    as God's champion, I, 130–32; XII,
        97–98
    guilt of, II, 152–53
    and Hercules, VI, 243–58
    heroism of, III, 195–96; VI, 255–
        57; VII, 45, 46, 69
    immortality of, III, 194; VI, 256–57
    as Israel's champion, I, 120
    and Job, XII, 131
    lamentations of, I, 118–19; XII,
        126–37
    and Manoa, I, 122–25, 131–32; II,
        198
    marriages of, I, 119–20, 123; II,
        154–55, 200; X, 25, 30; XII,
        106–07, 150–53, 155–56
    and Menelaus, I, 128–29
    mission of, II, 196–97
    and Moses, II, 7
    name of, XII, 97
    and Oedipus, I, 117–18
    in *PL*, VI, 245; IX, 50
    pride of, II, 161, 167; III, 193
    in rabbinical tradition, III, 185–

        200; IV, 199–200, 202–05, 211;
        VI, 247
    reason and sensuality of, III, 191–
        93
    in *The Reason of Church-
        Government*, IX, 47
    sensuality of, III, 186, 191–93, 197
    sonnets of, V, 149–50
    spiritual death of, II, 152
    spiritual education of, II, 149–74;
        XII, 118–19, 146–60
    suffering of, II, 150–52
    temptations of, II, 157–58, 159–64,
        166–67, 223–25; IV, 41–42; VI,
        71–72, 73; VII, 55; XII, 101–02,
        133–35
    as tragic hero, I, 117–33
    as type of Christ, III, 194, 196; V,
        79

Samson Agonistes
    accommodation in, VI, 97
    action and contemplation in, IV,
        44–45
    ambiguity in, II, 201
    Argument of, VII, 64–65
    authorial presence in, VII, 73–74
    biblical lament in, XII, 126–37
    biblical sources of, I, 118; II, 180,
        220; V, 79, 81–82; XII, 128–29,
        131–32
    blindness in, I, 117, 118–19, 124–
        25, 127; II, 222; V, 81; VI, 249
    catharsis in, II, 219–30
    Circe in, VI, 68–75
    and classical tragedy, I, 117–18,
        128–29
    color in, III, 58, 62
    comedy in, I, 122, 123, 130; X, 14–
        16, 27; XII, 92
    contraries in, VII, 44–45
    criticism of, VII, 49–50; XII, 118–
        19
    dating of, IV, 60; XII, 136–37

Samson Agonistes (cont.)
destruction of temple in, VII, 64–65, 71
dietary imagery in, II, 220–21
dragon in, IX, 48
as drama, VI, 243–44; VII, 49–76
and Eliot's works, XI, 116–17, 118–19, 120–21
ending of, XII, 121–22
as epic, II, 220
epigraph to, V, 8
and Euripides, VI, 248–57
fame in, X, 31
food in, II, 220–21
free will in, I, 132; VI, 255
genre of, XII, 92, 111
God in, VII, 59–60
hearing in, II, 177–79, 188
heroism in, III, 195–96; V, 131; VI, 255–57; VII, 45, 46, 69
hierarchy in, IX, 28–33
history in, XII, 122, 124–25
imagery of, II, 220–21; IV, 48–50; VI, 249; XII, 92, 98–100, 102
immortality in, III, 194; VI, 256–57
and Jewish tradition, III, 185–200; IV, 199–200, 202–05, 211; VI, 247
irony in, II, 169, 197, 198; V, 78; VII, 58; X, 15–16; XII, 108, 109, 159–60
kinship in, IX, 28–33
language in, II, 185, 186–88
law in, II, 186, 187; III, 187–98; XII, 150–53
liberty in, III, 193–94, 196, 197–98; XII, 141
light and dark in, II, 176–78, 193; VI, 249
love in, VI, 255
lyric verse in, XII, 94
marriage in, X, 25, 30; XII, 155–56
medical imagery in, II, 221–22, 225

Messenger's narration in, VII, 65–66, 73–74
monuments in, XII, 107–09
Mosaic law in, III, 187–98; XII, 154–55
multiple choice in, VI, 106–07
myth of exodus in, II, 7
names in, XII, 97
narrative elements of, XII, 92–93
noise in, XII, 100
and Old Comedy, XII, 95–97, 100–03, 109, 111
and *PL*, II, 179–81
and *PR*, II, 179; XII, 93, 104–05
parody in, VII, 44–46
patience in, II, 167–68, 190; VI, 71–72, 74–75
performance of, V, 4
phoenix in, II, 208; VI, 256; VII, 69, 71; IX, 51; X, 27
poet's calling in, III, 24
posture in, IV, 41
preface to, I, 116, 117; II, 215, 216–17, 222; X, 4
presumption in, II, 154–56, 159–60
prison imagery in, II, 181–82
Providence in, IV, 56–57
purification in, II, 226–27
and Puritan revolution, IV, 39–62
readers' reactions to, II, 175–76
reason in, II, 162, 163, 164, 173*n16;* III, 190–93, 196, 197–98
regeneracy in, II, 149–74; III, 191; VII, 55; XII, 141, 142
rhyme in, I, 53–54, 121–22, 133*n6;* XI, 5–6
servitude in, III, 193–94, 196, 197
sexual intercourse in, V, 223
silence in, II, 176, 183–84, 192
solar symbolism of, IX, 46–51
soliloquy in, VII, 53–54
sonnets in, V, 130, 148–51

and Sophocles' *Oedipus Rex,* XII,
103–04
sound in, II, 175–94
as spiritual biography, IV, 58
structure of, II, 223; X, 133; XII,
91–116
synesthesia in, II, 177–79, 189, 190
tempest imagery in, II, 188–89
temptation in, II, 157–58, 159–64,
166–67, 223–25; IV, 41–42; VI,
71–72, 73; VII, 55; XII, 101–02,
133–35
thought in, VII, 54, 55, 56, 57, 66
title of, II, 183–84; IV, 41, 44–45;
VII, 57
tone of, XII, 92
as tragedy, I, 115–33; XII, 103–04,
111, 121
as tragicomedy, X, 3–21
two plots of, VII, 50, 64
typology in, III, 194, 196; V, 78–82
victory in, VII, 63–64
vocation in, IV, 41–44, 47, 55, 57.
See also Chorus (*SA*); Dalila;
Harapha; Manoa; Samson
Samuel, Book of, as source for *PL,*
III, 177; IV, 210–11
Samuel, Irene, *II, 131–48; X, 177–93*
on comedy and satire, VIII, 121*n*17
on *PL,* VI, 96; VIII, 286–87
on *PR,* VI, 216
Sandys, George, VII, 296, 299; X, 38,
42
Circe in, VI, 36–37
—"The Minde of the Frontis-
peece," VI, 36
—*Ovid's Metamorphoses,* VII, 299
Sankey, Benjamin T., XI, 83
Sapientia-Fortitudo. *See* Wisdom
and strength
Sartre, Jean-Paul, IX, 4–5
Sasek, Lawrence A., on *PL,* IX, 88
Satan
and Adam, I, 103–07; X, 73–74;

XII, 86
and Almanzor, I, 55–57, 59
and Antaeus, XII, 243
as antihero, VII, 129
appeal of, IX, 8, 11, 82
and Beelzebub, I, 81–84; X, 65–70
biblical portrayals of, I, 75; XII, 20
as brother of Christ, IV, 7–8
Calvin on, IX, 269
as caricature, V, 80; VI, 217
changes in, I, 95–113
character of, I, 71–88
and Circe, VI, 55–57
as comic figure, I, 104, 106, 113
concupiscence of, VII, 296–98
as conspirator, I, 80–81; IV, 67–69,
72–76
and Dalila, XII, 99
and Death, I, 41–42, 84–85
"degradation" of, I, 69–70, 73–74,
77, 93–94; III, 105–06; V, 7, 8,
135–38; VI, 56–58; VII, 252–53;
VIII, 228–29
descriptions of, in *PR,* II, 98–99
despair of, I, 71–72, 80, 82–83, 85,
86
destructiveness of, IV, 32–33
as deviant, IX, 10–11
disguises of, I, 76, 79, 95–96, 110,
111–12
dissolution of, VIII, 165–207
and Eve, I, 103–07, 109, 110; V,
234–36; VI, 58–59; XII, 3–4, 10,
11, 12
evening described by, VI, 265
and faithful angels, I, 107–09
fall of, I, 47, 100–03; VII, 198–99;
VIII, 229–35; IX, 87–88, 268;
X, 65–66, 69–70
and fallen angels, I, 85–88, 109–10
false heroism of, I, 41–43, 56–58,
71–72, 73–75; II, 60; V, 9–10;
VIII, 184–86, 189; IX, 8
as fire god, IX, 74*n*97

Satan (cont.)
　　foreknowledge of, XII, 214
　　free will of, III, 104
　　and Gabriel, I, 42, 43; III, 106
　　at gates of hell, I, 6–7
　　as Gnostic, XII, 259
　　in gunpowder sermons, IV, 64–65
　　and Hermetic Man, XII, 15–16
　　and Hesperus, IX, 153
　　ignorance of, VI, 228–29, 235–36,
　　　　237–38
　　in infernal trinity, V, 145–46; VII,
　　　　39; IX, 23–24
　　ingratitude of, I, 98–100
　　inner hell of, V, 200
　　journey of, I, 11; II, 64–65; VII,
　　　　38; VIII, 6; IX, 81–82
　　kinship relations of, IV, 7–8, 10–11
　　language of, I, 35–37, 69–88, 71–
　　　　72, 79–80; II, 65–66, 67–68, 72–
　　　　73, 88; IV, 25–26, 29; VI, 14–15,
　　　　219, 220; VIII, 254–55, 256; IX,
　　　　130–31; X, 158–59
　　love of, I, 103–04, 105
　　manner of, in PR, IV, 181–82
　　and the moon, IX, 158–59
　　moral responsibility of, I, 100–01;
　　　　VI, 56
　　motivation of, IV, 207
　　muteness of, VIII, 256
　　and Napoleon, XI, x, 86, 87–89,
　　　　91–93, 95
　　in PR, II, 87–88, 95–99; IV, 180,
　　　　181–82, 183–84, 186, 187, 188–
　　　　89, 190, 191; XII, 253–66
　　and Pharaoh, II, 11, 19, 71–72
　　as Pharisee, XII, 262
　　and poet in PL, II, 59–82
　　posture of, VIII, 228–35
　　as predator, VII, 287–89
　　pride of, I, 8, 101, 107, 109; V, 13;
　　　　VII, 268, 296; X, 156
　　and Prometheus, IV, 102
　　quest of, II, 6

　　in In Quintum Novembris, IV, 63,
　　　　66–67, 68–69
　　and Raphael, XII, 38–39
　　as rebel, VIII, 216
　　recalcitrance of, VIII, 279–83,
　　　　285–87
　　remorse of, X, 73–74
　　republicanism of, II, 73
　　and Robespierre, XI, 89–91
　　role of, in PL, II, 59–82; V, 59–60;
　　　　VIII, 216–17
　　Romantic view of, XI, x, 83–85, 86,
　　　　88, 108
　　as satirical figure, I, 55, 56–58, 60
　　self-deception of, I, 8, 102, 110–11
　　self-knowledge lacking in, III,
　　　　104–07
　　self-pity of, I, 101–02
　　and serpent, II, 28–30
　　and Sin, I, 84–85, 175; VI, 110;
　　　　VII, 296–97
　　as Socinian, XII, 256
　　soliloquies of, I, 72, 73–74, 80–81,
　　　　97–107, 110–12; III, 104; V, 5,
　　　　11, 14; VIII, 285–86
　　as son, IV, 8
　　sonnets of, V, 135–38, 147–48
　　and Sophists, I, 74–75; VI, 217
　　and storms, V, 162–64
　　as tragic figure, I, 113; V, 616
　　and Tree of Knowledge, VII, 239
　　and Turnus, I, 32
　　tyranny of, IV, 24, 31, 129; V, 12
　　uncertainty of, XII, 255–56
　　view of hell of, VIII, 179–81
　　in War in Heaven, III, 173–74
Satire
　　in Animadversions, V, 89–90; VIII,
　　　　108–13
　　in Colasterion, VIII, 85
　　of heroic drama, I, 55, 56–58
　　in Marprelate, VIII, 104–06
　　Milton's, II, 113–18
　　in PL, I, 55, 56–58, 60; XI, 46

in *PR*, XI, 46

Satyr plays, X, 7, 8, 9, 11

Saurat, M. Denis, VIII, 186, 201
  on *Areopagitica*, VI, 86
  on Blake, VIII, 141
  on *PL*, II, 61–62

Savile, Henrie
  translation of Tacitus by, IV, 121
  —*The Ende of Nero*, IV, 130, 131, 132, 133, 134, 135

Scales, in *PL*, I, 42, 43

Scaliger, Julius Caesar, III, 38
  on epithalamium, V, 41, 48, 51, 52, 53, 54, 59, 62
  on pastoral, III, 44
  on style, III, 45–47, 49, 50
  —*Poetices libri septem*, V, 41, 48, 51, 52, 53, 54, 59, 62; VII, 170, 171–72, 179, 181, 184n13; X, 44

Scarlet Woman, VII, 304–05

Schaeph, Gerard, XII, 169–70

Scherer, Edmund, XI, 110–12

Scholasticism, Milton on, I, 17

Schuler, Johann, XII, 226

Schultz, Howard, VI, 90
  on *PL*, X, 99
  on *PR*, I, 52; IV, 178; VI, 86–89; XII, 213, 214

Science, in Milton, VII, 21

Scientific revolution, VI, 87–89

Scobell, Henry, XII, 184, 185

Scott, Thomas, XII, 169, 173

Scoufos, Alice-Lyle, VI, 113–42

Scripture. *See* Bible

Sculpture
  Adam and Eve as, VIII, 30–31
  in landscape, VIII, 27

Scylla, VII, 299–300
  and Charybdis, in *Comus*, VI, 108

Seaman, John E., on *PL*, VIII, 269

Sébillet, Thomas, on pastoral, III, 40–41

Second Bishops' War, VIII, 54

Second Coming, II, 5, 104; V, 105–06, 192

Second Defence. See *Defences*

Seed, in *PL*, III, 152–53; V, 171

Selden, John
  —*Uxor Ebraica*, X, 197

Self-deception, Satan's, I, 8, 102, 110–11

Self-esteem
  in *PL*, VIII, 235–38
  in *The Reason of Church-Government*, VIII, 243
  in *Second Defence*, VIII, 243–44

Self-knowledge, XII, 13–14
  Adam's, III, 107; V, 160–61; X, 95–96
  Calvin on, III, 106–07
  Eve's, III, 108–11, 113, 114, 115, 116–17
  in *Lycidas*, III, 3–34
  and Narcissus, III, 108, 112, 113, 114, 116–17
  in *PL*, III, 103–18
  Satan's lack of, III, 104–07

Self-pity, Satan's, I, 101–02

Sellin, Paul R., on *SA*, IV, 41

Selvaggi, XI, 4–5

Seneca, XII, 244–45, 247

Sensuality
  in *Comus*, IX, 26
  in *SA*, III, 186, 191–93, 197

Sermons
  on gunpowder conspiracy, IV, 64–66, 72–73, 75
  military imagery in, IV, 47–48, 49
  as source for *SA*, IV, 40

Serpent. *See* Dragon; Snakes

Servitude
  and brutishness, VI, 54–58, 66–69
  in *SA*, III, 193–94, 196, 197.
  See also Liberty

Servius, on pastoral, III, 40, 45

Sewall, Richard, on tragedy, V, 10–16

Sewell, Arthur, XII, 62

Sexby, Edward, IV, 57–58

Sexual intercourse
　Luther on, VI, 281
　in Paradise, V, 52–53, 223; VI,
　　277–84
　St. Augustine on, VI, 279–81
　in SA, V, 223
Sexuality
　in Comus, VI, 175–77; VII, 148–49
　in PL, I, 162–64; VI, 6, 265
Shade, III, 73; VIII, 37–38. See also
　Trees
Shakespeare, William
　Keats on, XI, 99
　and Milton, compared, V, 73–74,
　　80
　on order, IV, 21–22, 23
　as source for L'Allegro and Il
　　Penseroso, IX, 212
　tragedies of, V, 10
　on tragedy, V, 8–9
　—Hamlet, VII, 63, 72; X, 8
　—Henry V, XII, 203
　—Macbeth, V, 12; VI, 105; IX,
　　100
　—Othello, IX, 100
　—Pericles, VII, 249
　—Richard II, V, 8–9; VII, 55
　—Troilus and Cressida, IX, 212
On Shakespeare, V, 73; VII, 142–43,
　145; IX, 213
Shawcross, John T., II, 3–26; VII,
　127–63; VIII, 209–19; X, 39, 43
　on Milton's vocational choice, VIII,
　　41, 45, 48–49, 50, 61
　on PL, VII, 213; XII, 75, 79
Shelley, Percy Bysshe
　response to Milton of, XI, x–xi
　on Satan, XI, 85
　—Adonais, XI, x–xi
　—Alastor, XI, x
　—Defence of Poetry, XI, 78
　—Prometheus Unbound, XI, xi
"Shepherd," in Lycidas, III, 14–17,
　32

Shepherds
　in Comus, VI, 154–55
　and poet, X, 59
Sheppard, Sir Fleetwood, XI, 8
Sherry, Beverley, VIII, 247–66
Shumaker, Wayne
　on Lycidas, III, 62; IV, 157
　on PL, VII, 244
Sibbes, Richard, II, 54; IV, 53–54;
　XII, 32–33
Sicilian Muse, in Lycidas, III, 15, 50;
　IV, 153; IX, 238–39
Siciolante da Sermoneta, Girolamo,
　VII, 299–300
Sidney, Sir Philip, IX, 208
　on history and literature, II, 132,
　　143
　on Moses, VII, 212
　Paradise of, II, 42–43, 44
　on tragicomedy, X, 3–4
　—Apology for Poetry, X, 3–4
　—Arcadia, V, 44; VIII, 88
　—Defense of Poesy, II, 132, 143;
　　XII, 125
Sight, as metaphor for intellect, VI,
　188–90. See also Blindness
Silence
　as dissent, XII, 249
　in Lycidas, III, 9–11
　in SA, II, 176, 183–84, 192
Simmonds, James D., on Milton Stud-
　ies' tenth anniversary, XII, vii–xi
Simpson, Percy, on masque, VI, 144
Sims, James, X, 151
　on PL, II, 32
Sin, allegorical figure of, in PL, I, 77,
　175
　and Adam and Eve, VII, 289
　birth of, I, 99; VI, 110; VII, 296;
　　XII, 15–16
　and Dagon, VII, 44
　and Dalila, XII, 98
　and Death, I, 11, 84–85; V, 80;
　　VIII, 176, 178, 179–80

and Eve, IV, 11
in infernal trinity, V, 145–46; VII,
    39; IX, 23–24
kinship relations of, IV, 10–11
as predator, VII, 287–89
sonnet of, V, 145
transformation of, VII, 299
Sin
in *Areopagitica*, III, 130
in *De Doctrina Christiana*, VII,
    296
and evil, XII, 26–28
and freedom, VII, 8–9
and free will, XII, 50
in Kierkegaard, XII, 7–9
in *SA*, II, 154–56, 159–60
uncaused, X, 7–8
Singing-gift *topos*, VII, 172–74, 176,
    177
Sion College Presbyterian Synod, X,
    196–97
Sion Hill, II, 75–78
Sirens, VI, 69–70
in Tasso, VI, 28–30
Sirluck, Ernest, I, 167–68, 174, 182;
    IV, 101, 102; IX, 69, 206
    on *Doctrine and Discipline of
    Divorce*, X, 204, 205
    on *Tetrachordon*, X, 206
Sisto da Siena
    —*Bibliotheca Sancta*, XII, 223–24
Skepticism
    Milton and, VI, 99*n15*
    value of, VII, 6–8
Skinner, Daniel, IX, 250, 255, 256
Slakey, Roger L., on *Sonnet 19*, X,
    141–42
Smallenburg, Harry R., IX, *169–84*
Smaltius, account of Rakow Colloquy
    by, VIII, 196–97
"Smite," in *Lycidas*, II, 125
Smith, John, XI, 55, 72
Smith, W. Robertson, VII, 250, 253–
    54, 259

Snakes
    curse on, V, 205
    in *PL*, II, 27–35
    symbolism of, IX, 49–51
Socinianism, VIII, 193–202; IX, 263;
    XII, 256
Socinus, Faustus, VIII, 193, 194–95
Socrates, V, 8
Socratic dialogue
    in *PL*, IX, 89–101
    in *PR*, VI, 215–26.
    See also Plato
Solar symbolism, IX, 37–75. *See also*
    Sun
At a Solemn Musick, VIII, 56–57
    and *An Apology*, V, 106, 119
    regeneracy in, V, 103, 104, 107
    worship in, I, 170, 173
Soliloquies
    Adam's, V, 220–21, 222; VII,
        52–53; IX, 145; X, 70–75
    Christ's, VI, 233–35; VII, 197,
        200–01; IX, 266
    Eve's, V, 215–18, 219
    of Lady (*Comus*), V, 295–96
    in *Lycidas*, VII, 72
    in *PL*, I, 72, 73–74, 80–81, 97–107,
        110–12; III, 104; V, 5, 11, 14,
        213–14, 215–18, 219–22; VII,
        52–53; VIII, 259, 285–86; IX,
        145; X, 70–75
    in *PR*, VI, 233–35; VII, 197, 200–
        01; IX, 266
    in *SA*, VII, 53–54.
    See also Satan, soliloquies of
Sol niger, IX, 59–60, 63
Solomon, in *PL*, II, 78–80. *See also*
    Song of Solomon
Son
    as brother of Satan, IV, 7–8
    in Council in Heaven, III, 163–68,
        171
    in Creation, VII, 278–79
    as God's representative, IV, 29–32

Son *(cont.)*
  and Hermetic Demiurge, XII, 15
  heroism of, I, 43–44; II, 85, 90; V,
    23–24, 25, 27, 28; VI, 106; IX, 8
  judgment by, VIII, 274–75
  language of, X, 158
  mercy of, IV, 25
  mildness of, VI, 269–70
  in *PL*, II, 20, 27–34; III, 145; IV,
    29–32; V, 17, 169; VI, 187
  sacrifice of, VIII, 279
  Satan's skepticism of, XII, 255
  as son, IV, 8
  in War in Heaven, I, 23, 25–26;
    III, 174–75, 177, 178; IV, 71–
    72, 75–76; V, 132.
  See also Christ
Song of Solomon, VI, 186, 191; VII,
  283, 284, 287, 289–90
  as epithalamium, XII, 30
  hortus conclusus in, II, 22; VII,
    130; XII, 30, 34–35
  patristic exegesis of, XII, 30–32
  Reformist interpretation of, XII,
    30–31, 32–34
  as source for *PL*, XII, 29–30, 35,
    41
Song on May Morning, VII, 142–43
Sonnets
  in *Comus*, V, 152n2
  in *PL*, V, 129–47
  in *PR*, V, 130, 131, 147–48
  public, V, 147
  in *SA*, V, 130, 131, 148–51
Sonnet 1, V, 110; VII, 133, 142–43
Sonnet 2, VII, 143, 144
Sonnet 3, V, 129; VII, 143, 144
Sonnet 4, VII, 134, 143–45
Sonnet 6, VII, 144
Sonnet 7, III, 4, 23, 24; VII, 71, 136;
  VIII, 57; X, 151; XII, 199–200
  and *An Apology*, V, 110
  Milton's vocational choice in, VIII,
    41, 43–46

  and Pope's *Imitations of Horace*,
    VII, 35
  puns in, VIII, 45
  quoted in full, VIII, 44
  and *The Reason of Church-
    Government*, V, 113
Sonnet 9, III, 58; VII, 35
Sonnet 10, IV, 107
Sonnet 12, VI, 55
Sonnet 14, III, 56
Sonnet 15, VIII, 218
Sonnet 18
  biblical sources of, X, 175
  faith in, X, 167–68, 170, 175
  imagery of, X, 168, 171–72, 173–
    74, 175
  persona of, X, 167, 168
  as prayer, X, 168–70, 175–76
  quoted in full, X, 167–68
  syntax of, X, 168, 172–73
  tableau in, X, 172
  tenses in, X, 171, 173–74, 175
Sonnet 19, XII, 200
  biblical sources of, X, 144–49
  criticism of, X, 141, 142
  dating of, X, 149–52
  "fondly" in, X, 142–43
  forgiveness in, X, 162–63
  obedience in, VIII, 244
  as parable, X, 141–54
  patience in, X, 143, 144–45
  psychological development in, X,
    162–63
  quoted in full, X, 155–56
  "stand" in, VIII, 244
  syntax of, X, 143, 156–57
  vocation in, IV, 42
  and War in Heaven, X, 155–65
Sonnet 20, VII, 134
Sonnet 21, VII, 134
Sonnet 22, X, 115–16
Sonnet 23
  Alcestis in, IV, 143, 147–48; V, 76–
    77; VI, 182, 184–85; VIII, 153,

156–58; X, 111–12, 116–22, 127–39

analogy in, IV, 142–44

biblical sources of, IV, 145–47; V, 75, 76; VIII, 160; X, 124, 135

biographical approaches to, IV, 141–42; VI, 181–82, 186

blindness in, IV, 141, 142, 145, 146; VI, 185, 187, 188; VIII, 159–60; X, 116

"child-bed taint" in, IV, 143–45

color in, III, 62

criticism of, IV, 141–42

"delight" in, VI, 190–92

as drama of lost salvation, VI, 181–97

"embrace" in, VI, 192–93; X, 112–13, 122

and Euripides, X, 11–12, 116–19, 121, 124, 128–29

Hercules in, V, 76–77; VI, 184–85

heroism in, X, 113–14

imagery of, VI, 183

irony in, V, 75; VI, 192

Jewish tradition in, VI, 182, 185

light in, IV, 147

love in, VI, 183, 189–92

marriage in, IV, 146, 147

Neoplatonism in, VI, 182–83, 187–94

New Dispensation in, IV, 143, 144, 145–46

Old Law in, IV, 143–46

organization of, VI, 182

and Orpheus, X, 129, 132, 133

purification in, IV, 143–45; V, 75; VI, 185–86; VIII, 149–63; X, 119, 134–35

religious meaning of, IV, 142–49; VI, 181–97

sacrifice in, VI, 184–87

salvation in, VI, 181–97; VIII, 153; X, 119

simile in, X, 111–25

structure of, X, 127–39

subject of, IV, 141–42

syncretism in, VI, 183–84, 189

typology in, IV, 144; V, 74–78; VI, 183, 184–87, 194–95; X, 133–36

veil in, VI, 188–89; VIII, 159–60

Sophistry. *See* Rhetoric

Sophists, I, 174–75; VI, 217

Sophocles

heroism in, VI, 244–45

tragicomedy of, X, 9–11

—*Antigone*, X, 9–10

—*Electra*, X, 9

—*Oedipus at Colonus*, I, 117–18; X, 10–11, 14

—*Oedipus Rex*, V, 6, 7, 17; XII, 103–04

—*Philoctetes*, IX, 69

—*The Searchers*, X, 7

—*Women of Trachis*, VI, 244–45, 246

Sorbière, Samuel, I, 53

Sound

in *Lycidas*, III, 9–11, 15

in *Il Penseroso*, VIII, 13

in *SA*, II, 175–94.

See also Noise

Space, and time, I, 62

Speculum Virginum, VII, 304–05

Speech. *See* Language; Soliloquies

Spengler, Oswald, VII, 15

Spenser, Edmund, I, 26

Circe in, VI, 31–36, 78nn23, 24

on Clio, X, 44

evening in, VI, 262–63, 265

flowers in, III, 64

Hesperus in, V, 43

hymns of, VII, 168, 177, 180–81

muse of, III, 28

paradise of, II, 39, 41, 42, 43, 44

reason in, VI, 35

singing-gift *topos* in, VII, 173

as source for *Lycidas*, IX, 229–30

Wood in, VI, 146

Spenser, Edmund (*cont.*)
  —*Faerie Queene,* I, 46; II, 39, 41,
    42, 43, 44; III, 28; VI, 31–36,
    78nn23, 24; VIII, 76–77, 78, 80,
    86, 87, 89, 93–94, 113, 250; IX,
    197–98, 208, 210, 215–16; X,
    44, 52
  —"An Hymne in Honour of Love,"
    IX, 63
  —*The Shepheardes Calendar,* III,
    41; IX, 229–30; X, 37, 38
  —*Teares of the Muses,* X, 48
Sperry, Stuart, on Keats, XI, 104
Spirit
  as agent of Creation, I, 149–57;
    III, 30–31
  in *Areopagitica,* I, 150
  in *De Doctrina Christiana,* I, 148;
    III, 29; VII, 228–29
  in Genesis, I, 149, 150
  as guide to truth, I, 148–49
  in image of dove, I, 150
  and Moses, I, 148
  as muse, I, 147–50, 182–85
  in *PL,* I, 147–57; III, 29–31; VII,
    229–30; X, 54–55
  in *PR,* II, 85, 95; VI, 228
  in Tasso, III, 86.
  See also Attendant Spirit
Spitzer, Leo, IV, 142, 143, 146, 147;
    VI, 181–82, 183, 184, 185, 186,
    188, 189, 192
  on David and Christ, XII, 125–26
  on *Sonnet 23,* VIII, 150–51, 157,
    159–60; X, 127
Spivack, Bernard, X, 23–24
Sprat, Thomas, V, 225
"Stand"
  in *PL,* VIII, 221–46
  in *PR,* VI, 232
  in *Sonnet 19,* VIII, 244
Star of Bethlehem, XII, 217–22, 225–
    28
  in Milton, XII, 228–30

Stars
  in Blake's *Milton,* XI, 56–59, 60–
    61, 71
  in *Lycidas,* XII, 230
  in Nativity ode, IV, 169
  in *PL,* VI, 266–67
Stavely, Keith W., V, 269–87
Steadman, John M., I, 67–92; VII,
    3–27; I, 22; VII, 40; X, 53
  on apotheosis tradition, XI, 67
  on *PL,* VIII, 184–85; IX, 186; X,
    107–08; XII, 63
  on *PR,* IV, 180–81
  on *SA,* II, 190; X, 25–26
  on Satan, X, 178
  on Sirens, VI, 29
  on War in Heaven, I, 25
Stein, Arnold, I, 93–113
  on *PL,* I, 2, 12, 22; V, 27, 80; IX,
    93, 137, 142
  on *PR,* I, 52; IV, 190
  on *SA,* II, 183, 185, 188; VII, 64
  on War in Heaven, IV, 49
Stephanus, Charles
  —*Dictionarium Historicum,
    Geographicum et Poeticum,* III,
    68
Sterry, Nathaniel, XII, 188
Sterry, Peter, XII, 13–14
  —*A Discourse of the Freedom of
    the Will,* III, 113–16
Stillingfleet, Edward
  —*Origenes Sacrae,* VII, 245–46
Stoehr, Taylor
  on *Sonnet 19,* X, 143
  on *Sonnet 23,* VI, 194
Stoicism
  in Milton and Tacitus, IV, 129–
    30
  in *PL,* V, 17, 26–27
  in *PR,* XII, 241–45
Stollman, Samuel S., III, 185–200;
    IV, 195–215
  on Samson, VI, 247

Storms
in *PL*, V, 162–64
in *PR*, VIII, 26–27
in *SA*, II, 188–89
Stringer, Gary A., *X, 141–54*
Strode, William
—"Against Melancholy," VII, 83
Structure, defined, VII, 30–31
Style
and meaning, I, 1–3
Milton on, II, 113–18
Sublimation, IX, 58–66, 70
Sublime, in *PL*, VIII, 20; IX, 151–52
Submission
in *PL*, IV, 8, 14–16
and tyranny, IV, 120–21, 122–23, 124–25, 136–37
Suicide, in *PL*, VIII, 182–83; IX, 22
Summers, Joseph H.
on heroism, II, 157
on *PL*, III, 172; IX, 122, 132, 133, 137, 141, 142; XI, xii
on *SA*, II, 170; XII, 94
Sun
in Blake's illustrations for *L'Allegro* and *Il Penseroso*, VIII, 135–36, 138
in Blake's *Milton*, XI, 65
in *Comus*, XII, 230
in Nativity ode, IX, 44–46; XII, 230
in *PL*, V, 163; IX, 46, 52–56
symbolism of, IX, 37–75
Sundell, Roger H., *II, 83–101*
Sun gods, in Nativity ode, IV, 168–69
Surprise, in landscape, VIII, 25–28
Svendsen, Kester
on *PL*, I, 48
on *PR*, XII, 213
on *Sonnet 18*, X, 168
Swaim, Kathleen M., *II, 119–29; V, 155–76; IX, 121–49*
on *Lycidas*, IX, 224

Swan, John
—*Speculum Mundi*, IX, 157
Swedenborg, Emanuel, on Revelation, XI, 60, 61, 65
Swift, Jonathan
—*A Tale of a Tub*, IV, 90
Syncellus, Georgius
—*Chronographia*, VIII, 186
Syncretism
in *Comus*, VI, 129–30, 134, 136
in *Sonnet 23*, VI, 183–84, 189
Synesthesia, in *SA*, II, 177–79, 189, 190
Synod of Dort, XII, 55–56, 57, 58, 60
Sypher, Wylie, on heroic drama, I, 62

Tableaux
in *Comus*, VI, 157–58
in *PL*, VIII, 8, 27, 29, 32
in *Sonnet 18*, X, 172
The Table of Cebes, IX, 208–09, 213
Taboo, VII, 246–48, 252, 253, 257–61
Tacitus
effect of, in sixteenth and seventeenth centuries, IV, 117–19
influence of, on Milton, IV, 122–38
on liberty, IV, 118–19, 125–26
Milton on, II, 135
Milton's knowledge of, IV, 119–21, 125–26
style of, IV, 130–31
Talmud, Samson in, III, 186–87
Tasso, Torquato, I, 2, 13n2, 74
on action and contemplation, III, 84–85, 86, 89–91, 92–94, 96, 98, 100; VIII, 74–75
on baptism, III, 95
Circe in, VI, 28–31
on epic, I, 73
on knowledge, III, 94, 96–97
on Last Judgment, III, 94, 97–98
light in, III, 85–100
love in, VI, 28–31
and Milton, III, 84, 99–100

Tasso, Torquato (cont.)
  Moses in, III, 87
  muse of, III, 27–28
  nature in, III, 83–99
  Neoplatonism in, III, 88–89
  phoenix in, III, 96
  poet in, III, 87
  Spirit in, III, 86
  time in, III, 85, 89, 91, 93, 98–99
  trees in, III, 87–88, 97, 98
  —Aminta, III, 38
  —Discourses on the Heroic Poem,
    I, 70–71, 73
  —Il Forno, o della Nobiltà, VIII,
    99n10
  —Gerusalemme Liberata, III, 27–
    28; VI, 28–31; VIII, 74–75
  —Il Mondo Creato, III, 84–99
Tayler, Edward W., I, 16
  on SA, VII, 49–50; XII, 118–19,
    121
Taylor, Dick, Jr., on PR, IV, 180, 191
Taylor, Jeremy, on temptation, IX,
    271–72
Taylor, John
  —Nashe's Ghost, VIII, 107
Taylor, Thomas
  —Moses and Aaron, VII, 223, 224
Teilhard de Chardin, Pierre, IX, 69
Temple, Sir William, XII, 248
  garden of, V, 252, 253
Temple of Solomon, II, 75–76, 78–79
Temptation
  Circean, VI, 23–26
  in De Doctrina Christiana, II, 157
  in liturgy, VII, 192–93
  motif, I, 89
  in PL, II, 16–17; V, 19–20, 214–15;
    VI, 290–91; VII, 300; XII, 26
  in PR, I, 62; II, 88, 95–99; IV, 178–
    93; VI, 65–68, 218–21, 228; VII,
    43–44, 194–96, 202; IX, 264–
    65, 268–70
  in SA, II, 157–58, 159–64, 166–67,

    223–25; IV, 41–42; VI, 71–72,
    73; VII, 55; XII, 101–02, 133–
    35
Ten, symbology of, IX, 269–70
Tenure of Kings and Magistrates, V,
    270–71; XII, 147
  authority in, X, 186
  heroism in, VIII, 87
  law in, XII, 143
  Tacitus' influence in, IV, 124–25
Teresa of Avila, St., VII, 270
"Terrible," in landscape, VIII, 25–26
Tertullian
  on the magi, XII, 219–20
  on St. Paul's affliction, X, 146
  and Sonnet 18, X, 175
  —An Answer to the Jews, VII,
    234–35
  —De Pudicitia, X, 146
Tetrachordon, VI, 203–04; VIII, 84–
    85; XII, 155
  authority in, X, 183–84, 185, 186
  charity in, VI, 209, 210, 211
  law in, VII, 237, 260
Theocritus, III, 14
  —Hymn to the Dioscuri, VII, 173,
    174
Theodicy, XII, 50–55, 56, 59–60, 61–
    70
Theology
  ambiguity about, VI, 102–05
  covenant, VII, 236–37
  and poetry, I, 51–52
  Puritan, IV, 41–46, 55
Thomas, Northcote Whitridge, on
  taboo, VII, 248
Thomism, VI, 188. See also Aquinas,
  St. Thomas
Thompson, E. N. S., on Readie and
  Easie Way, V, 275
Thorndike, Lynn, XII, 217–18
"Thought," in SA, VII, 54, 55, 56, 57,
  66
Thucydides, II, 143–44; XII, 239

Thurloe, John, XII, 174, 175, 176, 177, 179, 181, 182, 183, 184, 185, 187, 189
Thyrsis, in *Comus,* IV, 156
Tiberius, XII, 237–38, 243–44
Tigris, X, 78–80, 84
Tillyard, E. M. W.
  on antiprelatical tracts, VIII, 65
  on Eve's dream, XII, 37
  on heroism, VIII, 76
  on history plays, V, 25
  on *PL,* III, 120, 121; VI, 64; IX, 89, 138; XII, 253
Time
  Christian or sacred, defined, VII, 189–90, 191–92
  and cyclic movement, II, 5
  end of, II, 8
  and landscape, VIII, 29
  liturgical or Platonic, defined, VII, 189, 190–92
  in *Lycidas,* III, 13, 26; IV, 159
  in Milton's unidentified verse, XII, 201, 204–09
  in myth of exodus, II, 7
  in Nativity ode, II, 110–11; IV, 166
  in *PL,* II, 23; V, 28, 42–43, 157, 171, 207–08; VIII, 215–16; IX, 87–88; XII, 76–79, 81, 85–86, 87
  in *PR,* I, 62–64; VII, 189–205
  in Revelation, II, 5
  and space, I, 62
  in Tasso, III, 85, 89, 91, 93, 98–99.
  See also History; *Kairos*
On Time, V, 103, 107; X, 122
Times Literary Supplement, debate on *L'Allegro* in, VII, 78–80
Timothy, Epistles to. *See* Paul, St.
Tiresias, VII, 137; XII, 103
Titian
  —*Bacchanal,* VIII, 31
Toal, M. F., VII, 194
Todd, Henry J., on *PL,* VII, 210
Toliver, Harold E., *IX, 105–20*

Tomkis, Thomas
  —*Lingua,* IV, 80
Touchet, Anne, Countess of Castlehaven, III, 211–12, 215, 217
Touchet, Mervyn, Lord Audley, Earl of Castlehaven, III, 203–05, 211–14
Tower of Babel, III, 150–51; XI, 94
Tradition
  in divorce tracts, I, 19–20
  elegiac, III, 11, 13
  Milton's adaptation of, I, 21–28
  Milton's attitude toward, I, 16–21
  nature of, I, 32–33
  rhetorical, IV, 109.
  See also Authority; Epic tradition
Tragedy
  Aristotle on, I, 70; V, 6, 7, 8
  Miltonic, VII, 51
  Milton on, I, 116, 117; II, 216; XII, 121
  in *PL,* II, 212–14; V, 5–17; VIII, 215
  purpose of, II, 213–14, 215
  Renaissance view of, V, 8–10
  in *SA,* I, 115–33; XII, 103–04, 111, 121
Tragicomedy
  in *Comus,* V, 20
  Greek, X, 7–14
  in *PL,* V, 19–23
  in *PR,* V, 25
  in *SA,* X, 3–21
  Sidney on, X, 3–4
Treatise of Civil Power, VII, 261; IX, 256
Treaty of Newport, V, 279
Tree analogy, in *PL,* V, 177–90
Tree of Jesse, V, 177–90; VII, 302–05
Tree of Knowledge, VII, 233–65; X, 97; XII, 6, 8, 36
  in *Areopagitica,* IX, 115–16
  and the cross, VII, 267–69
  in *De Doctrina Christiana,* VII,

Tree of Knowledge *(cont.)*
235–37, 254, 255
in Donne, VII, 268
ecclesiastical view of, VII, 254–55
as fetish, VII, 251–53
fruit of, III, 60; V, 166, 167–68,
214–15, 216–18, 219, 222, 223–
24
in iconography, VII, 298–99
as image, VIII, 14
in J text of Genesis, VII, 233
location of, VIII, 22–23
mythic associations of, VII, 249–50
in *PL*, III, 60, 124–28; VII, 237–
39, 240–42, 248–49
Renaissance exegetes on, VII, 234–
35
sacredness of, VII, 256, 258
St. Augustine on, VII, 248
Semitic view of, VII, 253–54
as taboo, VII, 247–48, 257–61
Tree of Life, VI, 104
in *De Doctrina Christiana*, VII, 248
ecclesiastical view of, VII, 254–55
fruit of, III, 60; V, 258
as image, VIII, 14
in landscape, VIII, 5–6
location of, VIII, 22–23
in *PL*, VII, 248–49
in *PR*, VI, 238
Trees
in *L'Allegro*, VIII, 15–16
in Paradise, V, 255, 256–58, 263–64
in *PL*, II, 40, 41, 44–45; III, 99; V,
224; VIII, 14–15, 35–36
symbolism of, VII, 154
in Tasso, III, 87–88, 97, 98
Trinity, I, 149
in Creation, VI, 103
in *De Doctrina Christiana*, XII,
254
infernal, V, 145–46; VII, 39; IX,
23–24
in Tasso, III, 87–88, 97, 98

Trinity manuscript, III, 15; V, 39–40;
VI, 167; VII, 146, 208, 214; VIII,
64; IX, 232, 233; X, 38–39, 60;
XII, 204
Triptychs, in Milton, X, 132–33
Of True Religion, X, 182
Truth
absolute, VI, 90, 91–92
in *Areopagitica*, IV, 97; VI, 90–91;
VII, 36–37; VIII, 86; IX, 6, 179–
82, 183, 196–97
in *De Doctrina Christiana*, VI, 86,
91–93
in *Lycidas*, III, 18–19, 25–26
Milton on, I, 17–18
modern theories of, VI, 87–89
in *PL*, X, 101
in *The Reason of Church-
Government*, III, 6–7
in *Of Reformation*, I, 17–18, 28;
III, 6
and rhetoric, I, 69–88, 90.
See also Accommodation
Tuckney, Anthony
—*The Balme of Gilead*, IV, 93
Tung, Mason, on *SA*, XII, 118, 127
Tupper, James Waddell, on Dalila, X,
28
Tusser, Thomas
—*Fiue Hundreth Points of Good
Husbandry*, V, 263
Tuve, Rosemond
on allegory, V, 79
on *L'Allegro* and *Il Penseroso*, VII,
82; IX, 212
on Circe, VI, 22
on *Comus*, VI, 176
on *Lycidas*, III, 9
on Nativity ode, II, 105–06, 108;
VII, 167, 173–74, 176, 177; IX,
44
"Two-handed engine" (*Lycidas*),
VII, 46; VIII, 48, 50; IX, 221–22,
235

function of, II, 122–24
interpretation of, II, 119–20
meaning of, II, 123, 125–27
Tyndale, William, VI, 121
Typhon, in Nativity ode, IV, 173, 174
Typology, II, 227
in Blake's *Milton*, XI, 63–65
defined, V, 69
in Dryden, XI, 12
and imagery, V, 67–85
and imagination, V, 72
in *Lycidas*, V, 74, 77; IX, 224
Milton on, V, 70
moon in, IX, 159, 163
in Nativity ode, IV, 170
in *PL*, I, 12; II, 76; V, 17, 74–75,
    186; VII, 209, 210, 221–30,
    268–69; IX, 143–44
in *PR*, V, 78–79; VII, 199; IX,
    261–75; XI, 12
in *SA*, III, 194, 196; V, 78–82
in *Sonnet 23*, IV, 144; V, 74–78;
    VI, 183, 184–87, 194–95; X,
    133–36
Tyranny
and Antichrist, VI, 129
and Catholicism, IV, 124
and reason, VI, 55
Satan's, IV, 24, 31, 129; V, 12
and submissiveness, IV, 120–21,
    122–23, 124–25, 136–37
and Tacitus' influence, IV, 118

Ulreich, John C., Jr., V, 67–85
on *Lycidas*, IX, 224
on *Sonnet 23*, X, 112, 127, 135
Uncleanness, VII, 257–60. *See also*
    Purification
Unreadiness
in early poetry, VIII, 55–60
in *Lycidas*, III, 8
Upon the Circumcision, V, 104
Urania, IV, 7; X, 35–36, 48–52, 57
in *PL*, I, 182–85; II, 66; V, 30;

VIII, 158, 263; IX, 159; X, 53–
    55, 57–61
in *PR*, X, 61
in Shelley, XI, x–xi
Uriel, I, 158–59
in *PL*, II, 65–66, 67; IV, 208–09
speech to Satan of, V, 146–47
"Urim," IX, 52–53
Uroboros, XII, 4–5
Ussher, Bishop James, IV, 64
Utopianism, in Milton, V, 270, 272–
    73

At a Vacation Exercise, VII, 138;
    VIII, 42, 72; XII, 231
heroism in, VIII, 52
imagery of, V, 92, 122
performance of, V, 4
water in, VIII, 16
worship in, I, 178
Vainglory
in *PL*, IV, 185
in *PR*, IV, 181, 183–84, 185–86,
    189
Valeriano, VIII, 157
Valla, Lorenzo, XII, 53
Van Doren, Mark, XII, 261
Vane, Henry
—*The Retired Mans Meditations*,
    VII, 234
Vaughan, Henry, IV, 124; VI, 189,
    194
—*Silex Scintillans*, II, 19
Vaughan, Thomas
—*Euphrates*, IX, 59
—*Magia Adamica*, IX, 59–60
Veil
in *PL*, IX, 152, 164
in *Sonnet 23*, VI, 188–89; VIII,
    159–60
Veritas, VI, 140n42
Verity, A. W.
on *PL*, I, 170; V, 43
on *SA*, XII, 91

Vestments, IV, 85–88
Vettori, Pietro, X, 187
Via, John A., V, 87–127
"Vicissitude," in PL, VI, 272
Vida
    —Christiad, I, 46
    —Hymns, VII, 173, 180
Villa Aldobrandini, VIII, 19, 27
Vincent of Beauvais
    —Speculum doctrinale, IV, 92
Violence, in PR, IV, 181, 182
Virgil
    catalogue convention in, I, 33–34
    color in, III, 56, 57, 62, 65, 68–69
    evening in, VI, 261–62
    heroism in, I, 38–41
    pastoral of, II, 45–46; III, 14–15,
        36–37, 38, 40, 42, 43, 47
    as source for L'Allegro and Il
        Penseroso, IX, 215
    as source for Comus, VII, 153–54
    as source for Epitaphium Damonis,
        VII, 153–54
    as source for PL, I, 31–43, 46–48
    —Aeneid, I, 31–50; III, 57, 62; V,
        132; VI, 262; VII, 197; IX, 153,
        215; XI, 11, 12; XII, 242
    —Eclogue 1, II, 45–46; VI, 261–62
    —Eclogue 2, VII, 153–54
    —Eclogue 4, IX, 238–39
    —Eclogue 6, VI, 261–62
    —Eclogue 7, VII, 154
    —Eclogue 10, VI, 261–62
    —Georgics, II, 46; III, 36–37
Virginity, VII, 148–50, 152. See also
    Chastity
Virtus, VI, 244. See also Areté
Visconti Hours, VII, 272
"Vision of Paul," IX, 229
Vocation
    in Catholic theology, IV, 42–43
    in Protestant theology, IV, 43–46,
        54–55
    in SA, IV, 41–44, 47, 55, 57.

    See also Milton, John, vocational
        choice of; Poetry
Voegelin, Eric, II, 8, 9, 10, 13
Vondel, Joost van den
    —Adam in Ballingschap, VI, 279;
        XII, 40
Von Gierke, Otto Friedrich, IV, 91–
    92
Vox Borealis, VIII, 107
Vulgate, VII, 102, 108, 109, 111,
    115–16

Waddington, Raymond, on Satan,
    III, 105–06
Waith, Eugene M.
    on Herculean hero, VI, 244
    on tragicomedy, V, 20
Waldock, A. J. A., III, 120–21
    on Fall of Man, XII, 6, 9
    on PL, I, 35, 36, 37, 69, 71, 72, 73,
        74, 77, 94; III, 136n5, 181n10;
        V, 80; VI, 64, 290, 293, 298; IX,
        89, 93, 95, 100
Walker, D. P., VIII, 194–95, 198,
    199–200, 200–01; XII, 54
Wall, John N., Jr., XII, 117–39
Wallace, John M., X, 211–12
    on Anthony Ascham, X, 195
Wallerstein, Ruth, on Areopagitica,
    IV, 108–09
Walls, in Paradise, VIII, 6–8, 9
Walpole, Horace, VIII, 9
Walther, Rudolph, VI, 130
Walwyn, William
    —Compassionate Samaritans,
        VIII, 86
Walzer, Michael, IV, 45–46, 48, 52,
    80
"Wander," in PL, II, 10, 68–70; IX,
    78–80
War, Puritan view of, IV, 48–50, 52–
    55
"Warfaring Christian," VII, 149;
    VIII, 100n22; IX, 197–98

War in Heaven, I, 26–27, 43–44, 87–88, 174, 175; II, 11, 14; III, 77, 124, 171–80; IV, 49–50, 69, 71–72, 75–76; V, 7, 132; VI, 6; IX, 161
  catalogue convention in, I, 36
  language in, X, 157–61
  as metaphor, I, 22–26
  and *Sonnet 19*, X, 155–65
Warton, Joseph
  evening in, VI, 260
  on *PL*, II, 37, 38; V, 250
  on *PR*, IX, 263
Wasserman, Earl, XI, 29
Water
  in *L'Allegro* and *Il Penseroso*, VIII, 13
  in *Comus*, VIII, 18
  in hell, VIII, 34
  in landscape, VIII, 16–19
  in *Lycidas*, VIII, 16–17
  in Nativity ode, VIII, 20
  in Paradise, VIII, 17–20, 22–23, 36–37; X, 58–59, 78–80
  in *At a Vacation Exercise*, VIII, 16
Waterfalls, VIII, 19
Watson, J. R., on *PL*, XII, 79
Webber, Joan, on *Of Reformation*, VIII, 78
Weber, Burton J., *IX, 77–103*
  on *PL*, XII, 76
Weber, Max, IV, 43
Weckherlin, Georg, XII, 174, 175, 184
Weemse, John
  —*The Pourtraiture of the Image of God in Man*, VIII, 249, 257, 263
Weese, W. E., on *Sonnet 19*, X, 144
Weismiller, Edward R., on *Lycidas*, IX, 222, 236
Weldon, Robert, XII, 143
West, Herbert F., Jr., on *L'Allegro*, VII, 84
Westminster Confession, XII, 61, 64

Weyden, Roger van den
  —*The Annunciation*, VII, 302
Wheeler, Thomas
  on *PL*, XII, 6–7
  on *Sonnet 23*, IV, 142, 148; VIII, 151
"When I consider how my light is spent." See *Sonnet 19*
Whitaker, Juanita, *IX, 185–201*
Whitehead, Alfred North, VI, 86–87, 88, 89, 95
Whitgift, John
  —*Defense of the Aunswere*, IV, 86, 87, 92
Whitman, Cedric H., on Homer, VII, 26–27n9
Whitney, Geffrey
  —*A Choice of Emblemes*, VII, 290
Wigler, Stephen, *X, 155–65*
Wilbur, Earl Morse, on Socinianism, VIII, 200, 201
Wilding, Michael, on *PL*, IX, 86
Wilhelm, Richard, XII, 3
Wilkenfeld, R. B., on *SA*, II, 169
Wilkenson, David, on *Comus*, III, 205
Wilkins, John
  —*The Gift of Prayer*, VIII, 249
Willet, Andrew, XII, 27
  —*Hexapla in Genesin*, VII, 234
Willey, Basil, on *PL*, III, 121, 197
Williams, Aubrey, XI, 29, 40
Williams, N. P., on St. Augustine, XII, 52
Williams, William Carlos, IX, 197
Williamson, Marilyn L., *IV, 141–49*
  on *Sonnet 23*, X, 127
Wilson, Edmund, on Sophocles, IX, 69
Wilson, John, on *PL*, XI, 83
Wilson, Thomas
  —*Arte of Rhetorique*, VIII, 248, 261–62
Wind, in *PL*, VIII, 169–70

Wisdom
  in *De Doctrina Christiana,* X, 170
  in *PL,* IV, 202–03; X, 57.
  See also Knowledge; Wisdom and
    strength
Wisdom and strength, VIII, 72–75,
  78–84, 86, 89, 90, 92–94
  in *An Apology,* VII, 50–52
  in *Areopagitica,* IX, 185–201
  in *Of Education,* VII, 151
  in *Ad Patrem,* VII, 51.
  See also Action and contemplation
Wither, George, XII, 125
  —*A Collection of Emblemes,* VII,
    270, 271
Wittreich, Joseph Anthony, Jr., *IV,*
  101–15; XI, 51–82
  on *Areopagitica,* IX, 199–200
  on Blake, VIII, 126
  on *PR,* XII, 22
Wolfe, Don M., on Milton's career as
  public servant, XII, 165
Wölfflin, Heinrich, III, 74; VIII, 10,
  11, 16
Wollebius, Johannes
  —*The Abridgement of Christian
    Divinitie,* IX, 254
  —*Compendium Theologiae
    Christianae,* VII, 255
Wollstonecraft, Mary, IX, 12–13
Woman Wandering in the Wilder-
  ness. *See* Lady Wandering in the
  Wilderness
Women
  freedom of, XII, 11–12
  Kierkegaard on, XII, 9–10
  Milton on, IV, 3–18; VI, 5–6; IX,
    11–13, 16–33; X, 26–28; XII, 21,
    22 (*see also* Dalila; Eve)
  as temptation, VI, 38–39.
  See also Criticism, feminist
"Wonder," in *PL,* IX, 133
Wood, Anthony à, IX, 251
Wood. *See* Landscape, in *Comus*

Woodcock, Katherine, IV, 141; VI,
  186; VIII, 150, 152–53, 159, 161
Woodhouse, A. S. P., VII, 43
  on *L'Allegro* and *Il Penseroso,* IX,
    210, 213–14, 215
  on Dalila, X, 23
  on *Elegy 5,* IX, 71n23
  on Milton's vocational choice, VIII,
    41, 43–44, 46
  on Nativity ode, II, 105
  on *PR,* IV, 186; VI, 216; XII, 255
  on *Ad Patrem,* X, 40
  on *SA,* II, 153, 179
Woolrych, Austin, on Milton's career
  as public servant, XII, 166, 177,
  180, 188
Word of God, II, 13, 118; V, 184, 185
Wordsworth, Christopher, XI, 78
Wordsworth, William
  Arnold on, XI,113
  and Coleridge, XI, 86–87
  Keats on, XI, 100
  on Milton, XI, 69
  Milton's influence on, XI, ix–x,
    83–98
  on *PL,* V, 130
  on Satan, XI, 83–98
  —*The Borderers,* XI, 84, 89, 94–95
  —*The Convention of Cintra,* XI,
    87–89
  —*Poems Dedicated to National
    Independence and Liberty,* XI,
    95
  —*The Prelude,* XI, ix, 89–92
  —*Thanksgiving Ode,* XI, 92–93
Work, in Paradise, V, 158–60, 262–
  64; VI, 6, 7–8; VII, 285–86; IX,
  111–12
Work ethic, IV, 43–44
World parents, myth of, XII, 4–5
Worship
  Milton on, I, 170–74, 178–83
  in *PL,* I, 149, 167–77; VII, 282,
    283–85

and poetry, I, 176–82
Wotton, Henry, IV, 131
Writer. *See* Poet; Poetry
Wundt, Wilhelm
—*Elements of Folk Psychology,*
VII, 258–59
Wyclif, John
—"De Papa," IV, 86

Xerxes, I, 11

Yeats, William Butler, I, 5, 13n7
—"Easter, 1916," I, 101
Yost, George, X, 77–91
Young, Thomas, VIII, 55; X, 36, 42,
43, 44
in *Elegy 4,* V, 108

Zanchius, Hieronymus, on rule of
charity, VI, 204–05
Zeal, Milton on, I, 178–79, 180
Zechariah, as source for *PL,* III,
172–73
Zephon, I, 107–08; III, 105, 106
Zeugma, in *PL,* VII, 108, 110, 111,
116, 119
Zeus, VI, 110; X, 5–6
Zevio, Stefano da
—*The Madonna in a Rosegarden,*
VII, 293–94
Ziegler, Hieronymus
—*Protoplastus,* V, 36n25
Zorobabel, VIII, 89
Zwicky, Laurie B., XII, 197